CO-AMB-765

FACING THE PITTSBURGH STEELERS

FACING THE PITTSBURGH STEELERS

PLAYERS RECALL THE GLORY YEARS OF THE BLACK AND GOLD

Edited by SEAN DEVENEY

SPORTS
PUBLISHING

Sports Publishing books may be purchased in bulk at special discounts for sales promotion, corporate gifts, fund-raising, or educational purposes. Special editions can also be created to specifications. For details, contact the Special Sales Department, Sports Publishing, 307 West 36th Street, 11th Floor, New York, NY 10018 or sportspubbooks@skyhorsepublishing.com.

Sports Publishing® is a registered trademark of Skyhorse Publishing, Inc.®, a Delaware corporation.

Visit our website at www.sportspubbooks.com.

10 9 8 7 6 5 4 3 2 1

Library of Congress Cataloging-in-Publication Data is available on file.

Cover design by Tom Lau
Cover photo credit: Associated Press

ISBN: 978-1-61321-927-0
Ebook ISBN: 978-1-61321-928-7

Printed in the United States of America

CONTENTS

INTRODUCTION

BACK IN THE summer of 1988, a team made up of former Cowboys went to Pittsburgh for a flag football game featuring almost a dozen Hall of Fame NFL alumni. Roger Staubach was there, as were Tony Dorsett, Cliff Harris, and Drew Pearson. Though Terry Bradshaw could not attend, Franco Harris suited up, as did Joe Greene, Lynn Swann, and John Stallworth. It was organized by linebacker Andy Russell, and was expected to be a relaxed, charitable affair designed to give older fans a trip down memory lane.

It was more than that. The Cowboys, twice vanquished by the Steelers in Super Bowls X and XIII, sought to exact some measure of vengeance. The Steelers, playing in front of their Pittsburgh fans, would allow no such thing. The limitations of flag football were ignored. Injuries prevailed. "I guess we got a little carried away, on both sides, competitively," Staubach recalled.

But, as Cowboys defensive lineman Larry Cole put it, the game went exactly as it should have. "No team got your competitive juices flowing like the Steelers. They were just so damn good. You always saw beating them as a measuring stick. Even in flag football."

What's funny about talking to former opponents of the Steelers—and not just opponents, but those who were among the most reviled in franchise history—is that they all seem to come back to the same point. And that is, no matter how much players might have wanted to beat the Steelers, no matter how intense the disdain for their rough-and-tumble ways, no matter how fervent the charges of dirty play might have been, those who faced the Steelers over the years have a universal respect for the franchise.

In the pages that follow, there are tales of spitting Steeler players, players who wanted to fight entire teams, players who were foul-mouthed and ill-intentioned, even a player who wielded a screwdriver on the playing field. But just about every player and coach who faced the Steelers—in their dynasty years, in the 1980s AFC Central battles, in the dynasty reboot of the 2000s—was left with the same impression. For all their much-discussed underhanded tactics, everyone loved playing the Steelers. From the Rams to the Bengals to the Vikings, there was a respect factor for the Steelers that was arguably unmatched with any other NFL team.

Little wonder. The Steelers have won six Super Bowls, the most in NFL history. They've appeared in eight Super Bowls, tied for the most in the league. They've gone 590-530-20, and have a sterling playoff record of 34-23. Their peak era, the mid-1970s, featured a team that boasted nine Hall of Fame players, plus a Hall of Fame coach, Chuck Noll, and Art Rooney, the owner who also made the Hall of Fame. Yes, eleven Hall of Famers connected to that one team.

But over the years, another impression has been left: The Steelers typically reflect the values of their indefatigable city. They work hard. They prepare. They can withstand adversity. And they've generally been honorable gentlemen.

"That was the thing," said former Dallas defensive lineman Larry Cole, who faced the Steelers in two Super Bowls in the 1970s and again in the Cowboys-Steelers charity game. "They were such good guys. I mean, years later, you might still want to hate them, because they won two Super Bowls we felt we had a chance to win ourselves. But you go to dinner with them, and you laugh with them, and you see they're just like you. They were great guys. You can't hate them."

Indeed, there has been much to love about the Steelers over the years. In putting together this book, the goal was to shine a light on the aspects of the team that not only made them successful, but that made the city of Pittsburgh—and the players who faced them—enjoy, respect and even love the Steelers.

Section 1

THE BEGINNING

CHAPTER 1

BUILDING BLOCKS

THERE WAS A time, after the 1975 season, when Steelers great Ray Mansfield, a lineman in the NFL since 1963, was seated on an airplane with linebacker Bill Bergey, a veteran with the Eagles. Mansfield had won his second Super Bowl ring and, even at age 35, was going to come back and play another year. Bergey asked him why. "I have three sons," Mansfield said. "I would like to win a ring for each of them." Bergey laughed as he remembered. "I played in the NFL for 12 years," Bergey said. "All I got was a conference championship ring. Ray wanted to go for three of the big ones."

That sums up what happened to the Steelers over the course of a few short years. In the 1960s—indeed, even before that—the organization was considered something of a joke, having routinely flubbed in the NFL's draft or, worse, making shrewd picks of players like Johnny Unitas in 1955 and Len Dawson in 1957, only to let them walk from the team in favor of middle-aged quarterback Bobby Layne. It was not an outfit run with foresight and discipline and was considered little more than a hobby for dapper Pittsburgh sportsman Art Rooney. Well before he was tallying his progeny's fingerwear, Mansfield was expressing his disdain for playing for Pittsburgh and told Steelers historian Abby Mendelson that when he was traded from Philadelphia in 1964, the Steelers were "pitifully out of shape" and added, "I did not want to come to Pittsburgh. They were the joke of the National Football League."

But even if they weren't so serious about winning, the Steelers always let their opponents know they were there. They'd gained a reputation going back to the 1950s for rough-and-tumble play, and it would be no surprise to their contemporaries that the famed 1964 photograph of legendary quarterback Y.A. Tittle, helmetless on his knees during a game as tassels of blood dangled from his forehead and cheek, was taken on the field in Pittsburgh. That spirit of pugnacity remained with the Steelers through a series of coaching changes and carried into the 1970s, when the talent level caught up with the team's physicality. Over the course of the decades, the stories of the great games and moments in Steelers history have piled up, mostly from the perspective of the victors, who were very often the Steelers themselves. But here, we will unpack stories of Pittsburgh football from the perspective of the others—those who faced the Steelers over the years.

If one player were to be chosen as the forerunner of what was to come for Pittsburgh football, it would be Hall of Fame tackle Ernie Stautner, who was just 6-1 and 230 pounds but played 14 seasons, made nine Pro Bowls, and played through countless injuries, missing only six games in his career. "I gotta be mean," Stautner once said. "At my size, I can't afford to play any other way. Unless I'm meaner than these big guys, unless I can intimidate them, I'd have no chance in the world against them." Even after he left the Steelers, Stautner's style of play resonated in Pittsburgh, and if the Steelers as a team have had an identity that has been passed through the generations, it could likely be traced back to Stautner.

Bob Lilly

Defensive Lineman

Team: Dallas Cowboys, 1961-73

After Stautner stopped playing, he coached the defensive line for two years in Pittsburgh, then spent one year with the Redskins before becoming Tom Landry's defensive coordinator in 1966—a position he held until 1988. It was in Dallas that Stautner began working with tackle Bob Lilly, who was already midway through his Hall of Fame career and had gone up against Stautner's Steelers several times.

THE FIRST THING I remember about Ernie was we had this tackle named Bob Fry. He came to Dallas in the (expansion) pool in 1960. Of course, all the teams gave up players in a pool that made the Cowboys, since they had no draft choices because they were formed after the draft. Bob Fry used to tell George Andrie and myself in practice before we played Pittsburgh, which we did twice a year, he said, 'Just hit me in the head as hard as you can. Slap me upside the head. Butt my head. Hit me with your forearm, because that's what Ernie's going to do to me all day.' I remember George telling me, 'This guy's crazy. He wants me to hit him in the head all the time.' I said, 'Wait till we play the Steelers, and you'll see why.'

One time at the Cotton Bowl, back when the hash marks were much closer to the bench, Don Meredith was pretty close to our bench and we could hear it: They were just killing him. Ernie and those guys were just mauling him. And after a while we heard Meredith call the play, and instead of calling it on 'Hut one, Hut two!' he started calling it on fruit. I don't remember the exact fruit, but it was like, 'Apples! Oranges! Pears!' and they snapped the ball on Pears. The Steelers guys were laughing so hard, and I believe they called timeout. They were really laughing over there, and they never did try to hurt Don again. They never tried to hit him upside the head or anything. After Ernie retired and came to Dallas as our defensive line coach I asked him about it and he said, 'Well, we took that as Meredith begging for his life.' He said Meredith was always funny, and Bobby Layne had pity on him too, because they were both from Texas. So he said, 'We decided not to try to kill him anymore.'

Ernie was a smart guy. He pretty much knew, from the way people lined up and everything, what they were going to do. He wasn't real big. But he would just pulverize the guy across from him. He would hit you. He would hit you with a forearm. He would really beat you down. Ernie didn't give ground, and they didn't run his way real often. You just didn't fool him on the run. He was pretty unbeatable. When he was rushing the passer he would do the same thing. He'd hit you right in the head with his forearm. Then he would get away from you and try to do the same thing to the quarterback. Back in those days we ran 60-65 percent of the time. Ernie, they'd try to double-team him or trap him, but they couldn't go one-on-one with him. They'd send fullbacks at him, but Ernie would murder those fullbacks. He knew they were coming, and he would just strike them.

When Ernie got to training camp (as a coach), the first thing he did was show us how to hit the two-man sled. He got on the back of it, and he told us how to hit it with our forearms. So we would hit it, and he'd say, 'You look like a bunch of babies hitting it with your forearms.' So he got back there, and one of us stood on it. He said, 'This is how you do it.' *Bam!* He didn't start by swinging his forearm at it. He started with his fists down at his sides and came up with his forearms and with his wrist hit that sled. Well, behind the pad, there's about a quarter-inch-thick piece of steel. He hit his middle knuckle on that steel, and he looked at it and it was starting to turn blue and swell up immediately. So he just did it again, and the bone came right through the skin. And so, they took him down to the hospital. This was during two-a-days, and he was back in practice that afternoon. His arm was kind of elevated and I said, 'Does it throb, Ernie?' And he said, 'You're damn right it throbs.' And we didn't say anymore. He had our attention from then on.

I learned a lot about the Steelers from Ernie. He had an incident once where he was supposed to get a Novocain shot in his ankle or knee, but they put something else in there that was for another organ in your body. Whatever it was, Ernie was dying on the table. He had

Last Rites while he was lying on the table. But Ernie, he was so tough and so strong that he came out of it, and by halftime he suited up and played. This was the kind of mode these guys had. Ernie, he went from Boston College to the Marine Corps, fought in the South Pacific, then came back and finished his college.

Ernie was an inspiration to us. I met a lot of those guys from Pittsburgh in those days, and they were all pretty gritty. They were tough. That's one thing they still have up in Pittsburgh, that attitude. The fans have it. The history is there. When Ernie's family had his funeral in Dallas in 2006, all of us old guys were there. Joe Greene came in. He came in after all of us had been seated. A lot of us got up and said a few words. I said, 'When Ernie was playing with the Steelers, our offense feared him, because the Steelers on defense were rough—rough and tough. He was such a fine man and really taught us an awful lot about football, and I thought Ernie really had a lot to do with the Steelers' success. Because those guys like him passed down that hardnosed, don't-give-up, don't-quit football.' Later, Joe Greene got up and said, 'I came here, and I didn't know if I'd be welcome or not.' (He knew he really was). But he said, 'Ernie Stautner was one of those who passed down the toughness and represented Pittsburgh.' He talked quite a bit about Ernie's legend, and a lot of the other players they had.

It was interesting to hear Joe say that.

Bill Bergey
Linebacker

Teams: Cincinnati Bengals, 1969-73; Philadelphia Eagles, 1974-80
   Before the start of the 1970s, the Steelers had a 35-year record of 157-253-18 and had finished in first place only once, finishing last 10 times.

They were, without a doubt, the joke of the NFL, but with the passing of the 1960s came the rise of televised football and the merging of the upstart AFL and the Steelers' NFL—plus the lucrative Super Bowl that followed the pro football season. That provided a strong incentive for Pittsburgh's venerable owner, Art Rooney, to start taking his team more seriously as a moneymaker. After years of giving little thought to the men he chose to run his team, Rooney began putting more serious football professionals into place, starting with coach Chuck Noll and personnel man Dick Haley, and soon after built a powerful team around the likes of Joe Greene, Mel Blount, Jack Ham, L.C. Greenwood, Terry Bradshaw, Franco Harris, Lynn Swann, John Stallworth, Jack Lambert, and Mike Webster. All ten of those players, plus Noll and Rooney, are in the Pro Football Hall of Fame.

Bill Bergey had a very good view on the turnaround of the Steelers from an annual disappointment to unmatched gridiron heights. First, he played college football against Bradshaw while he was at Louisiana Tech. Then, as a division rival with the Cincinnati Bengals, Bergey witnessed firsthand the rise of the Steelers and the folklore that grew up around them.

IN 1967, I played for Arkansas State, and we played a game at Louisiana Tech, which had a young quarterback named Terry Bradshaw. I just thought he was going to be awesome. We had a good defense, but the antenna did go up when you saw him play and how he could throw, and I thought he would be somebody we would be seeing in the NFL. It was the same year that Mean Joe Greene and Jon Kolb were drafted, 1969. I was the same year as they were. But I remember being impressed with Bradshaw right from the start in college, and he was just a gifted, gifted quarterback. We played him tough, but you could see when he threw the ball deep, he had a much bigger arm than most quarterbacks.

I remember those games, not so much with Cleveland, not so much with Houston, but the ones with the Steelers, because they were a bunch of tough sons of guns. I've got to tell you, the best way I can explain it is, football players don't really feel pain, you don't hear a lot of football players saying *ouch* or anything like that. We'd take our shots and go about our business. But the Steelers were different. When the Pittsburgh Steelers hit you, it hurt. It was just unbelievable. Mike Webster, for one, he was as good a center as I ever played against, God bless his soul. He was a guy who just would not give up on a play, not give up on a block. It could have been 20 degrees below zero, and he would be out there, no sleeves on, and everyone would look at him and just know he was a tough one. The one thing I remember about Mike Webster more than anything was that he never quit on a play until the whistle blew. He might have had my butt blocked into the third row, but he was not going to stop pushing me until that whistle blew. He was just a tough, strong son of a gun. I really think he was the toughest center I ever played against.

Jon Kolb, he was a great lineman and just really strong, he was into weights ahead of most guys. You know how he used to get ready for the season? He used to split rocks with a sledgehammer. He would swing a sledgehammer and split rocks. That is what we all heard. If it was not true, it did not really matter, because if you heard it, it was sort of intimidating, right? Some guys had other jobs in the off-season. But whatever you are doing in the off-season, this guy is splitting rocks.

I will tell you something about the two running backs, Rocky Bleier and Franco Harris. I have a lot of respect for Franco, I have respect for what he accomplished. I would not mean to be disrespectful of him. But it was just the way my body matched up against his body, I would love to play against a guy like Franco Harris every single week. I thought Larry Csonka from the Dolphins was the hardest hitter as a running back, I thought O.J. Simpson and Walter Payton were the two guys who were the flashiest and most elusive and maybe the hardest to bring down. But I never had any problem tackling Franco.

Rocky I had more trouble with. He was a little rascal who bugged the daylights out of me. He gave me a lot more trouble than Franco did. Bleier was a little like, when you hit him, it stung. He was not a big guy but he had a muscular body, he had been in Vietnam. He was a smart guy, too, I heard him give a couple of talks over the years, and he is impressive. But it was always tough to tackle him, he was like a bug that just kept stinging you.

Lee Calland

Defensive Back

Teams: Minnesota Vikings, 1963-65; Atlanta Falcons, 1966-68; Chicago Bears, 1969; Pittsburgh Steelers, 1969-72

Lee Calland spent the first part of his career with the Vikings, then went to Atlanta in the expansion draft in 1966. He bounced from L.A. to the Bears but finally joined the Steelers in 1969, giving him an insider's look at the way Chuck Noll and Art Rooney quickly reshaped the Pittsburgh roster. He faced the young, tough new Steelers daily in practice. Calland had so much faith in the outlook for the group that when he left Pittsburgh after 1972, he tried to write their future success—and a Super Bowl ring—into his contract.

IT WAS BAD at first, but it didn't last long. You had guys like Soup come in—Mel Blount, we called him Soup. You could see Ronnie Shanklin come in. Smitty, Dave Smith, he came in. Jon Kolb and Sam Davis and Jim Clack, big strong guys, muscle people on that offensive line. And on the defensive line, L.C. Greenwood and Joe Greene. I always wanted to play more man coverage, but at the time, that is when cover-2 was really heavy. But with that defensive front, they could put pressure on a quarterback so quickly that you knew they were going to play man-to-man eventually because they could. You could stand in the receiver's shoes playing man-to-man with a defensive line like that, there weren't but two moves he could make because that was all he had time for. But it was only later that the Steelers began playing man-to-man.

L.C. Greenwood, we used to call him Hollywood Bags. At one time, it was rumored they were going to trade him to L.A. He was going out to Hollywood. So it was Hollywood, and get your bags, because you're traded. Hollywood Bags! They made a smart decision not trading him, of course. On the other side, it was Mad Dog, that's what we called Dwight White. It was just a great front four, those guys. Bags was such a good athlete, he could just run around in there—when they would run trap plays on him, he was so good he would run around the trapper. It was not the right technique, the technique in cover-2 was to make the thing bounce outside and the corners would be there on the outside with the linebackers there on the inside, and you got the guy for no gain or for a loss. Hollywood was the only guy who could go around the block and still be athletic enough to make the play on the ball. I remember one day in practice, Bags did it, ran around the trapper. The next guy up was a backup, and when it was his rep, he did the same thing as Bags, ran around the trapper. Charles (Noll) came up to the other guy and said, 'Hey listen, you can't do that, that's not what we teach.' And the guy said, 'But hey, I just saw L.C. do that.' And Chuck said, 'Yeah, but you're not L.C.'

Jack Ham was a really smart linebacker, but he stole a pass from me once. We were 20 or 30 yards downfield and at the time, you always made a little extra money as a defensive back for interceptions. So I was downfield, and the receiver is running a deep out on me, and I step in front of him. I am thinking, 'OK, I have this one.' But guess who is there, stepping in front of me? Jack Ham! I wanted to fight him. I said to him—it was his first year, he was just a rookie—and I said, 'You realize how much money you just cost me?'

But then later, it occurred to me, he might have that in his contract, too. But I would not be mad at Jack Ham. Jack played in front of me, on my side, that year, and he was good right away, he saved my butt a bunch of times.

They got so many talented people, such great athletes, so fast and they worked hard. They were young, but if they made mistakes, it was because they were trying too hard and just did the wrong thing. It was never that they were dogging it or not giving the effort. I left Pittsburgh in 1972 and I remember the year before, I told Charles they should probably trade me, I meant it. I said, 'Hey, it is time for Soup to play.' We had guys sitting on the bench who should have been playing and starting, and I had gotten hurt and it just seemed like it was time. But I took pride in them. I took pride in watching Mel Blount do what he did in his career. He would have been great anyway, but I tried to help him a lot. He was a really talented guy, but I just tried to show him what I knew. He was from Southern University, a small school, but you could tell right away he could play. What really helped Mel, too, was getting with the offensive linemen, guys like Jon Kolb. Those guys were big into the weights and I mean, they could bench press the world. Mel got into that, and he became very, very strong.

When I was getting ready to leave pro football, I talked with Art Jr., and I tried to get it in my contract, get like a future payoff. I told him, 'Look, you guys have Bradshaw now, and he is going to be a great quarterback who will win a lot of games for years and years and years. You got all these young guys.' I told him, if he didn't want to pay me the money I want to make now, how about we make a deal where if Pittsburgh gets to the Super Bowl, I want some of that Super Bowl money and a ring? I knew they were going to win one or more than one, but I knew I wasn't going to be there. He said, 'Lee, I can't do that!' I said, 'Why not? You can do anything you want here!' But I knew how good they were going to be, you could see it was going to come together.

CHAPTER 2
ENTER MEAN JOE

IN 1968, THE Steelers had finished 2-11-1, and with the fourth pick in the 1969 draft, fans were looking for new coach Chuck Noll—officially hired one day before the draft—to make a splashy pick that would breathe life into a moribund franchise. Noll knew what he wanted and chose a defensive lineman from North Texas State named Joe Greene. The reaction was a collective yawn. Pittsburgh sportswriter Jack Sell led off his draft story by noting, "The Steelers yesterday drafted a guy named Joe as their No. 1 choice in the combined NFL-AFL college player lottery. That failed to send a single season ticket buyer to the club's office in Hotel Roosevelt. … When news of Greene's selection was made public, it got a rude reception from Steeler rooters, who have watched the local club foul up in the past." But Noll pointed out that the Steelers had the worst pass defense in the NFL the previous year and defended his selection. "Most of the pro scouts rate Joe Greene from North Texas as the greatest defensive lineman in action last season," Noll told reporters. "He's 6-4, 274 pounds and very fast for his size. Most important, though, is that he wants to play. I met Joe personally at North Texas when I was talent scouting for the Baltimore Colts. One of his strong points is rushing the passer and from the films I have seen, that was one of Pittsburgh's big weaknesses last season."

Greene became a Steeler in that draft, but over time, he would become so much more. He was the one player most closely associated with what it would mean to be a Steeler under Noll. With hindsight and an impressive resume—10 Pro Bowls, two Defensive Player of the Year awards, four Super Bowl championships, and a Hall of Fame selection—it's safe to say Noll was right about Greene.

Rod Rust

Coach

Team: North Texas State, 1967-72

Rust, a lifer in the coaching business, was thirty-eight years old when he became the North Texas football coach in 1967. Among the talented players on his roster was Joe Greene, who was the anchor of a defense that led the Mean Green (his collegiate mascot provided the genesis of the Mean Joe nickname) to a 23-5-1 record in a three-year span.

THERE WASN'T ANY question in anyone's mind in Denton, Texas, that he was going to be a great pro football player. It was written all over him. The other players loved him. From the time I got down there, all of our games had scouts there. The practices, too. Chuck Noll would come down when he was working for (Don) Shula in Baltimore, he really took an interest in Joe. He liked our program, I guess, because he also drafted one of our defensive backs, Chuck Beatty, and (wide receiver) Ronnie Shanklin, too, a year later.

We used to have one-on-ones, a defensive lineman going up against an offensive lineman and just working on technique, which was kind of a charade in Joe's case because he could have just run over our offensive linemen if he wanted to. Paul Draper was our 190-pound center, he was supposed to block Joe one-on-one, and Joe had 90 pounds on him. Joe just stood there and clawed him with his hands, pushed him aside, and that was it. So I said, 'Go again.' I wanted more of a fight. It was supposed to be an explosive drill. So Draper did the same thing and Joe did the same thing, and I said for a third time, 'Go again.' That time Draper got into Joe a little bit and Joe used a move to beat him. That was what the drill was supposed to be. After the third time, I said, 'OK, next up.' And Paul Draper, he was dripping with sweat, and he said, 'Phew!' and sort of figuratively wiped his brow, like, 'I survived that.'

But that was the thing about Joe, he could have embarrassed him right there and run right over him. He didn't want to do that to his teammate, though. Joe was not a bully at all, and to be honest, he would hold back against some teams and then play his best games against the best teams. If we were playing a smaller team that we could handle, he would try to make sure other players could make plays, too. He never took a game off, he played well enough for us to win, but he was not going to show off. He was not going to find the cripple on the other team's line and abuse him the whole game. If we had a lead, he would become invisible, let his teammates shine. Joe had a tremendous amount of dignity and pride to him, and you learned that about him even in college.

In Greene's rookie year, 1969, the Steelers opened with a win, then lost 13 straight to finish 1-13. It was a taxing year for Greene, who wasn't even halfway through his first NFL season and had already lost more games than in his entire college career. Frequently, he would let his emotions get the better of him, and he became known for having a short fuse. "It's like a nightmare," Greene told *Sporting News* writer Rich Koster. "Everything goes against us, and there's nothing we can do." But Greene was already showing signs of greatness, and went on to win the Defensive Rookie of the Year Award.

Ed White

Offensive Lineman

Teams: Minnesota Vikings, 1969-77; San Diego Chargers, 1978-85

Ed White had come out of California in 1969 and was drafted in the second round by the Vikings. White did the usual tour of college All-Star games before the draft and in the process got to know Joe Greene as a fellow defensive lineman. White would switch to the offensive line in the NFL, but at one point in his first year in the league, the fact that he'd had an opportunity to befriend Greene turned out to be a lifesaver—almost literally.

AS A ROOKIE coming out of college, I was in the East-West Shrine game, I was the same year as Joe, and we were both defensive tackles. We got to know each other a little bit. We played that game, and we went to our teams after the draft. Early in the preseason, I was a backup, and the left guard, whose name was Jim Vellone, he had been the starter for eight years or so. He and Joe were having a pretty good tussle. And Jim was getting the best of him, because I think he said something that was pretty offensive. So our coach took Vellone off for the next series, and put me in. I run on the field with the offense and get in the huddle, go to the line of scrimmage and as I am walking up, I notice something in Joe's hand. He had come back on the field with a screwdriver. And I'm going, 'Hey Joe! It's me, Ed!'

I think I was down there holding my jersey up so that he could see it was a different number. His eyes were like huge saucers in red, I was not sure he had a grasp of who was in there. But I think what happened was his teammates kind of shuffled him off the field before anything could really happen.

Lee Calland

Having been with several organizations before joining the Steelers in 1969, Calland had seen plenty of players in practice and behind the scenes. But he knew immediately that, in Greene, Pittsburgh had a future star.

JOE WAS EVERYTHING they thought he was going to be. You had to be tough, and he was tough. When you would go into the line on a safety blitz or something like that, you'd go in there and, wow, what a terrible sound he would make when he hit someone. It was just different; it was such a loud *pop*. But Joe was made for that. He really was mean, that nickname was good for him. On passing plays, when the pass was thrown, Joe would be locked up with the guy who was blocking him and he would turn—like everyone would do—and see where the ball was going. But Joe would raise up an elbow and knock the guy who was blocking him in the face with his elbow. By accident, of course, by accident.

Joe used to, when he first came in, there was Joe and a guy named Charles Beatty, we called him Chuckie B. They were both from North Texas State. Chuckie knew Joe really well and he was another defensive back, so he told me how to handle Joe. Joe's first year, he was so young and eager to hit somebody, he would be out there chasing the pulling guard. They would pull the guard and run a sucker play to the other side right behind him, and Joe would leave a hole by chasing the guard because he wanted to hit somebody. But that meant you had a big, 230-pound fullback untouched by the time he got to the secondary. You don't like that as a defensive back. Joe was a young guy, and he was just chasing everyone around, he had not learned to play smart. Beatty told me to watch for that because I would have to step up and make those tackles on the fullbacks. Finally, one game Joe did that, and I had to make the tackle. I went into the huddle and I said, 'Joe, look, if you chase that guard one more—I won't use the explicit term I used—one more time, and that fullback comes through, I am going to let him keep on going and that is going to be on you.' He stopped chasing that guard after that. He was so fast and strong, but he got better and better the smarter he got.

He made an impression right away. We were in Chicago in the middle of that first year (1969) and Dick Butkus hit Bags, hit him so hard he knocked him out over by our bench. Butkus was sort of standing there, standing over him, you know, almost taunting. Joe went up to him, said something to him, and spat right in his face. I thought it was going to be the fight of the century. But Butkus didn't want any of that. He turned around and walked away.

Joe made it his team. We were up in camp in Latrobe and we were up in the rooms playing poker at lunchtime. Fats comes in—that is what we called (defensive tackle) Ernie Holmes, I think he was a rookie then—he comes in and says, 'I am going to the store to get some sandwiches and stuff like that, does anybody want anything?' And so we go through, we tell him get this and get that and gave him money to go. Joe does the same thing, makes his order, gives him some money. Fats comes back, and he has got everybody's order but Joe's. And we all knew what was happening. Fats and Joe played the same position, and they had a thing about who was going to be starting, who was going to be the big dog and all of that stuff. So Fats didn't bring back Joe's order and they start arguing and it is getting heated, Fats is on one side of the table and Joe is on the other. Those rooms were not very big and so they were real close and they were getting into it. I stepped in between them because that's more than

500 pounds altogether between the two guys. Thank goodness they calmed down because who knows what could have happened.

Jackie Slater

Offensive Lineman

Teams: *Los Angeles Rams, 1976-94; St. Louis Rams, 1995*

Jackie Slater was a third-round pick of the Rams in 1976 who would go on to play twenty years in the NFL and was inducted into the Hall of Fame in 2001. But long before that, coming out of Jackson State, Slater was eager to prove his worth to pro scouts and participated in that year's college All-Star game in Chicago, which happened to be the final time the NFL held an All-Star game in which college players went up against the previous year's Super Bowl champions.

WHENEVER I SEE Joe now, I put my hands together and I bow to him. Because the first time I played against Joe Greene was in the college All-Star game. I played against him, it was the last college All-Star game. I was lucky the game got canceled because it was raining, and it started with the lightning and the thunder, so they called it off. Now, when they called it off, the happiest guy in the building, or in a 100-mile radius, was me. That was because Mean Joe had already tried to take off my head with a couple of knees to the chin. He told me at the beginning, 'Hey, listen, this is a preseason game, lay off my legs.' I was thinking, when someone starts talking to you, they're just trying to use it to their advantage. I was going into the draft, I was trying to get a job. So there was a play, I went down and I got to his legs, I could feel my shoulder pads bouncing off his legs. I was on the ground, and I was getting ready to get up off the ground, and there was Joe's hand, he was grabbing my shoulder pads. I was thinking, I really got him that time, he is helping me up. As soon as I got to my feet, he kicked me across my shins and my knee, about three times. He tried to break my knee, he really did. I laugh about it now, to this day, I pay homage to him when I see him. But he was trying to put me in the hospital.

Tom Jackson

Linebacker

Team: Denver Broncos, 1973-86

Jackson, now an analyst for ESPN, got to know Joe Greene over the course of his 14-year NFL career with the Broncos, especially in three trips to the Pro Bowl, where he was Greene's AFC teammate—though he'd long heard about Greene during his time in college at Louisville, which was in the same conference as Greene's North Texas Mean Green. He got an especially up-close view of Greene during the 1977 playoffs, when Greene famously punched Broncos lineman Paul Howard in the gut, causing him to go hard to the turf.

I CAME FROM THE Missouri Valley, the same conference as Joe, though he was before me. But he was a legend when I got to Louisville, when they were talking about North Texas State. He was legendary. I came into the league with a kind of respect for him even beyond what he'd done as a Steeler. I had been hearing Joe Greene stories for years before that in college. He was the guy everything revolved around as far as the Steel Curtain goes, but he could also be funny when it came to his aggressive nature, his reputation. Everybody remembers him hitting Paul Howard in the gut in that playoff game. But from our perspective, what we saw was this: From the sideline, the play takes place, the ball goes downfield, we look up and we see Paul lying on the ground, writhing in pain. We can't figure out what happened to him, he is a tough guy, it is not like him to be on the ground unless something is really wrong. We look up at the screen for the replay, and we see it—Joe just got mad and just punched him, right in the gut. Like, a haymaker. I don't know if Paul was ever the same after that.

So, we get mad. We start yelling from our sideline, the whole team. There is some profanity there. We're all yelling, but we are yelling at Joe, the consensus was 'You're a real a—hole!' You know, for doing that. Joe hears that, and he starts marching, toward our sideline. All of us are yelling. But he starts coming at us. He literally is going to take on the entire Denver Bronco team. And I don't remember a single guy who didn't back up a little bit when they saw Joe approaching. I know I did. He was really going to come and take us all on. It is funny now. We said all these things, just in reaction. And here comes Joe, saying, 'OK, let's discuss this further.' And all of us stopped talking right there. I was thinking, 'Oh my gosh, he is coming here to deal with all of us at once.'

We knew on the field, he could be really tough. One of the stories we all heard about him was that Ernie Holmes was on the sideline while the defense was on the field. And (defensive coordinator) George Perles went up to Ernie and said, 'Well, why are you not on the field? What's wrong with you?' And Ernie said, in a soft voice, 'I was freelancing too much and Joe told me to come out and not to come back in until he said it was OK.' Perles told him to go back out, but Ernie wouldn't until Joe let him back. If you played against Joe, you heard that story and you said, 'Oh yeah, we get it. It's Joe.'

We knew Joe was really mean. That nickname was maybe more apropos than any in the history of football. He was mean. Not only on the field, but he was mean to everybody. He was mean to kids, even.

Publicly, I mean—it was his persona. I remember exactly how this happened, we were at another Pro Bowl and it was just after Joe had done the commercial, the Coke commercial (in 1979), handing the kid his jersey. Joe would usually walk right past all the kids. But now, all the kids at the Pro Bowl that year had seen that commercial, so now they just think, well really, Joe is a nice guy. He wants to give all the kids his jersey, right? He's not so mean.

End of the first practice, all of these kids, you would not believe how many. A flood of children. And we're thinking that these poor kids, Joe is going to be mean, going to walk right past them, because we were used to it. But there were so many of them and they were all yelling, 'Joe! Joe!' And they broke him. He couldn't be mean. Joe went over and he was signing jerseys, talking to them, being nice. We were all laughing saying, 'They broke him! They broke Mean Joe!' A bunch of kids saw him be nice in that commercial and now they're all expecting him to be nice, and he did not know how to handle it, except to be nice. They broke him. The funny thing is, I used to tell these stories around Joe. He would get annoyed. He wanted to keep his reputation. I would tell a story and he would say, 'Stop that!' He did not like people telling stories about him. I would say, 'Joe, they're all true!' I never saw anything like him, and there has never been anybody, I think, who would not want him on their team. The one thing about Joe is, it wasn't just the way he played, it was the way he was going to make everyone else play. He wasn't going to allow you not to play well.

He was just a different dude.

Bob Lilly

Like many of the Cowboys, Lilly had gotten to know Greene off the field a little because Greene had hailed from just outside of Dallas and spent his off-seasons there. Lilly is a Hall of Famer himself, so it was little surprise that, back in the early 1970s, when it came to contract negotiations with the Steelers, Greene and his attorney, Bucky Woy, turned to Lilly for salary advice before signing a new contract with the Steelers.

JOE WAS PROBABLY in his second or third year and he was really showing great ability. His friend, who was an attorney in Dallas, they met me at a club, and it was one of the clubs on top of a building in downtown Dallas. And, they were trying to figure out what Joe should ask for salary. The attorney wanted me to evaluate what we thought of Joe Greene. I told him that our offense has watched Joe a lot and I've watched Joe Greene a lot, and that I believe he's going to be a perennial All-Pro, and probably, if he doesn't get hurt, will be in the Hall of Fame. Obviously he did attain all those things and he's in the Hall of Fame and we're friends. He was a great athlete, first of all. He and Merlin Olsen were about the same size, a little bigger than me. Joe was very good about beating the zone block, he was really fast and he became a good pass rusher. He had the athletic ability and was smart, and he had good balance and good agility. He was quick off the ball. He did everything you'd expect of somebody and more, because he had more ability.

I remember once when we were playing them he just flat ran over the lineman over him, and the blocking back, and just creamed our quarterback. I thought he was going to knock him into the ground. He was like a steamroller. I thought, 'These guys are tough. We are in a war out here.' That made us tougher. Every time we played them, Coach Landry said, 'Put your helmets on tight because these guys will hit you.' When we played them, that week in practice we really went after the offensive linemen because we thought they needed to be toughened up.

Larry McCarren

Center

Team: *Green Bay Packers, 1973-84*

Greene was in his fifth season in 1973 when Larry McCarren was drafted by the Packers as a long shot lineman out of Illinois. Eager to find a spot on Green Bay's roster, McCarren took every preseason game seriously, including one against Greene and Pittsburgh. McCarren wound up playing twelve NFL seasons and had another encounter with Greene at the end of his NFL time.

WHEN I WAS a rookie, we were playing an exhibition game against the Steelers, and I was a 12th- round draft pick, so all I am trying to do is make an impression. I've got to hustle on every play like it's the Super Bowl. On one play, I hit Joe Greene late on a play. It wasn't that bad but it was after the whistle. And it was Joe Greene, it was 1973, he was already on his way to the Hall of Fame at that time, and I certainly knew who he was. But I hit him late on the play and when I did it, I realized it was him and it was, 'Whoops!' He turned around and grabbed me by the collar and looked at me. He has me there and he probably sees the fear in my face, and he goes, 'You're just a rookie trying to make the team, aren't you?' And I said, 'Yeah,' really quick. He just nodded and let me go, like he respected the situation I was in.

But then fast-forward eight years or so later, and we are playing Pittsburgh, and I can remember this—they used to play in these offset lineups, where Joe would be cocked out outside of the center and stuff like that. We had one run-blocking scheme, I had to reach him and get him cut on run-blocking plays. And with where they had him lining up, your only real chance was to get to him and try to cut his legs. I could do that, it was the only way

I could get him down, but at this time, eight years later, I would go to cut him and after the play he says to me, 'Hey, stay off the legs, will you?' It was funny, he was near the end of his career. But it went from respecting me as a rookie to saying, hey, respect me as a fellow veteran and stay off the knees. Over time, things like that change.

CHAPTER 3

IMMACULATE

	1	2	3	4	OT	Final
Steelers	0	0	3	10		13
Raiders	0	0	0	7		7

Nearly every native Pittsburgher knows the particulars. December 23, 1972. Three Rivers Stadium. Twenty-two seconds to play. AFC Divisional round playoff vs. the Oakland Raiders. Fourth-and-10, Pittsburgh 40-yard line. 7-6.

Those are the basics when setting the stage for what remains the greatest—and perhaps still the most controversial—single play in NFL history. Set against the backdrop of the Steelers' playoff desert (one appearance, in 1947, a 21-0 loss to Philadelphia), the stunning comeback win for Pittsburgh, starring Franco Harris catching a ball centimeters above the turf after a pass from Terry Bradshaw to Frenchy Fuqua was defended by Jack Tatum and ricocheted back in Harris's direction, became known as the Immaculate Reception.

The play marked a turning point for Chuck Noll and his new program in Pittsburgh, which saw Noll shed all but seven of the players he inherited when he got the job in 1969. In 1970, the team had opened Three Rivers Stadium, which for all its faults—bland, cookie cutter, covered in tightly stretched Astroturf—was thoroughly modern at the time and a luxurious upgrade over their collegiate-level digs at Pitt Stadium, and the ramshackle Forbes Field before that. The Steelers had improved from one win in Noll's debut year, to five wins, then six before breaking through with an 11-3 mark in 1972. That was the first year that Pittsburgh's defense became dominant, ranking second to the Dolphins in points allowed (171) and leading the league in turnovers (48) and yards allowed per play (4.2 yards). And it looked, against the Raiders, like the defense would hold, as the Steelers clung to a 6-0 lead until backup quarterback Ken Stabler led an improbable Raiders drive for a touchdown and a 7-6 lead with 1:13 to play.

Just 51 seconds later, and the Steelers were desperate, facing fourth down on their own 40. Curt Gowdy called the play on NBC's broadcast as Terry Bradshaw took the snap: "Last chance for the Steelers. Bradshaw, trying to get away. And his paaaass is … broken up by Tatum. … Picked off! Franco Harris has it! And it is over! Franco Harris caught the ball and it is a touchdown! Five seconds to go!"

There were three major points of controversy on the play. The first was whether anyone on referee Fred Swearingen's crew had even seen the play live, or did they lean on a de facto replay by allowing Art McNally, the supervisor of officials, who happened to be in the press box, to confirm the play's legality after he looked at replays. This was Oakland coach John Madden's big gripe in the days (and years) after the Raiders loss. Second was whether Harris had made a legal catch, because the ball was very close to hitting the turf for an incomplete pass when Harris grabbed it. Finally, the most-debated point: whether the ball first struck the oncoming Jack Tatum or Bradshaw's intended target, running back Frenchy Fuqua. If it hit Fuqua first, under old NFL rules, a fellow offensive player could not touch the ball next and Harris's catch would have been disallowed.

After what seemed an eternity of deliberation, the referees ruled that Tatum touched the ball first and that Harris caught the ball before it hit the turf. Despite the controversy, the final score stood. Officially, the Steelers won their first-ever playoff game, 13-7, on a 60-yard pass from Bradshaw to Harris.

Tom Flores
Assistant/Head Coach

Teams: Oakland/Los Angeles Raiders, 1972-87; Seattle Seahawks, 1992-94

Flores played ten years as a quarterback for Oakland, Buffalo, and Kansas City before getting into coaching with the Bills. He returned to Oakland as part of John Madden's staff in 1972 and would eventually take over the Raiders job for Madden in 1979. He was posted in the press box when Harris made his catch.

THAT WAS MY first year back with the Raiders, my first year there as an assistant coach. I was up in the box, and we saw the play as it was happening, and you could not help but be mesmerized a little because it was like the whole thing was in slow motion. We just needed to knock the ball down and we win the game. But all of a sudden, there is Franco Harris running with the ball and I said, 'How the hell did he get the ball?' When I saw the ball carom off of Fuqua and Tatum in their collision, it was hard to tell who hit the ball. The momentum came from Jack's end of it, but did he hit it or did Fuqua hit it? I could not tell and all of a sudden, Franco is in the end zone. Now, did he catch the ball legally? Or did the ball touch the ground? There was a lot for the officials to go over.

But I looked around at the crowd, they were going crazy and people were jumping from the stands and onto the field. I thought, there is no way they're going to be able to overturn this. If they overturn this, the people will go crazy and we won't be able to get out of this booth alive. Fortunately, we had black jackets on like the Steelers had, so if it came down to it, we could have turned them inside out and they would not have seen that Raiders logo on them. But they didn't overturn it, and we were just in shock. Even if there was replay, I don't think they had enough to overturn it, it would be something that we'd just have to live with.

We have over the years looked at all the footage of it, we have to relive that play every once in a while when it comes up. NBC had a lot of different angles on it and we went through all of them and there is just no way you can tell what happened there. It was illegal in those days for the offensive guy to touch it first and for another offensive player to catch the ball. That would have meant the play was dead where Fuqua touched it. So for it to be a legal play, Tatum had to touch it first. But to this day, you can never be sure. I will say that I heard from a pretty reliable source that Fuqua had a big bruise on his biceps where the ball had hit him. That was a pretty reliable source and, you know, there would not be a bruise there if it had hit Tatum first.

The other thing was that nobody tackled Franco after the play. Everybody just stood there, because everyone thought the game was over. If you watch it, our defense does not even react to Franco Harris until it is too late. And even before that, we should have had Bradshaw for a sack on the play, we had two guys just miss him. That would have been the end of it. But our team just stopped because it looked like the ball had bounced off the ground. Jimmy Warren was the last guy who saw Franco running and went to make a play on him, tried to catch him and get a piece of him, but by then he had a full head of steam going. That was the game.

Lee Calland

Calland's career was winding down, and 1972 was his final year playing in the NFL. But he had been helping defensive back Mel Blount along and was still part of the team when the Steelers faced the Raiders in that fateful postseason game.

I WAS THERE FOR the Immaculate Reception, I was injured, but I was on the sideline, I had my back injury. There was nothing I could do but cheer real hard for them.

I was standing right there, I saw it all. It was a legal play. Frenchy Fuqua came across to catch the ball, his arm was out. Tatum came in and he hit the ball and he took Frenchy's head off at the same time. The ball went up, it went right up and out like a rocket, and Franco was standing right there. It went right into his hands, it must have been about two or three inches off the ground when he grabbed it. I was so excited, I was there running down the sideline with him. You look at the film, you will see a guy with an Afro, black jacket and all, running step for step with him. That was me. The great thing about that, we were in the locker room, and we were jumping up and down screaming. Chief was standing there and he had tears in his eyes. He had to come back into the locker room because he had left the field thinking we had lost, he was so upset. He didn't see the play. It was such a surprise to him, when we came in screaming, you could see his face change, and it was like, 'Wow.' It was a great experience.

Mike Siani

Teams: Oakland Raiders, 1972-77; Baltimore Colts, 1978-80

Mike Siani says that he first realized that, as a Raider, he hated the Steelers, "when the ball hit the ground and Franco Harris picked it up and ran it into the end zone for a touchdown." Siani was a rookie starting at wide receiver in 1972, and said he had an ideal angle from which to judge whether Terry Bradshaw's errant pass had hit the turf before Harris made his catch. Siani was a key part of a Steelers-Raiders rivalry whose roots could be easily traced to the touchdown that ruined Oakland's postseason run back in 1972.

I HAVE SEEN THAT play for the last 40 years. I was not on the field, I was on the sideline, but I saw the ball hit the ground. Phil Villapiano was my roommate on the road, and I ask him all the time, he was responsible for covering Franco Harris on that play, man-to-man coverage. That was the defense. Every time I see him, I bust his balls and say, 'Hey, why didn't you cover him?' And he always says, 'For the thousandth time, I didn't cover him because he never came out of the backfield, if he would have come out of the backfield, I would have covered him. But he just stood in the backfield and the ball just happened to fly right back to him.' And I always tell him, you should have covered him anyway, you should have tackled his a– in the backfield.

I stood there with one foot on the field and one foot off the field, because it was fourth down and John Madden had just gotten the offense back together and said, 'OK, let's go back in, run one play and let's get the hell out of here.' As soon as I saw the ball flying back in the direction of Bradshaw, who had just thrown it, I said, 'OK, game's over.' Then all of a sudden Franco's got the ball and he is running down the far sideline into the end zone for a touchdown and within 20 seconds, there were thousands of people on the field. You don't see that in the NFL. Maybe in high school or college, where they carry the goalposts off, but not in the NFL. Thousands and thousands of people on that field within 10 or 20 seconds. The first thought in my mind was, get off the field and get someplace safe, because there were all these lunatic Steeler fans on the field. The locker room was like a morgue. No one knew what to say or do. It was just, 'What just happened out there?' None of us had ever been through that before, none of us had ever seen that before. Probably in the history of the league, that play never happened before and never happened since.

In, I would say it was about 1975 or 76, we were at Joe Namath's football camp in Connecticut, where Joe had this camp and kids stay overnight, like 600 kids during the week. Phil and I were there, teaching the kids. At night, they're showing NFL Films, the old movies, to the kids. They're showing the highlights from the

Vikings-Steelers Super Bowl in 1974 to all these kids, and it is on this big movie-projector screen like they used to have. They're showing a highlight of Franco Harris running the ball, and Phil, the lunatic he is, gets out of his chair and runs and rips the screen down like he is tackling Franco, and completely destroys this movie-theater screen. You've got 600 kids sitting there going, 'OK, what are we supposed to do now? We can't watch the film anymore because there's no screen. One of the camp coaches just tore it off the wall.'

About two or three years ago, I was at the Pro Bowl in Hawaii, I was working for the New Orleans Saints. I'm crossing the street, and who do I see but Franco Harris. Now Franco and I have known each other a long time, we played in college All-Star games together, so since 1971—'Mike, how are you doing?' 'Franco, good to see you, blah, blah, blah.' He says we should get together for dinner, and I say sure, we had dinner that night. For two hours, I kept asking him, 'When are you gonna tell the world that the ball hit the ground?' He never answered me. He would never answer me, no matter how many times I asked him.

By the way, I did not know that the stadium in Pittsburgh was so big, because it seems like two million people in Pittsburgh were at that game that day. Everybody you talk to from Pittsburgh tells you they were at that game. Every citizen in Pittsburgh. There was a time, I was talking to a Steeler fan, we were talking about the Immaculate Reception, and he says, 'Well, it's got to be true that he caught it because they have a statue of it at the airport.' I said, 'Oh, OK, that proves it.'

Professor John Fetkovich

There are films that appear to show—though no one can be certain— that the pass from Bradshaw, after it ricocheted, did not hit the ground.

Even if that were the case, it would not be enough to stop the Immaculate Deniers, who say that the real violation took place at the collision of Tatum and Fuqua. The two appeared to arrive simultaneously at the ball, and if it did hit Fuqua first, the play should have been blown dead. That's where Prof. John Fetkovich, a professor emeritus at Carnegie Mellon University, comes in. Beginning with a call from a writer at the New York Daily News *in 1997, Fetkovich took an interest in applying physics to the Immaculate Reception. With a brick wall and a football, Fetkovich conducted experiments chucking the ball, discus-like, against the wall and measuring both the speed of the ball heading toward the wall and the speed coming off after it hit the wall. He also had views of previously unseen camera angles of the game, allowing for precise measurements. According to Fetkovich's calculations, the only way the ball thrown by Bradshaw could generate enough return speed to carry it as far as it went to reach Harris was if the ball was struck cleanly by an obstacle moving in the opposite direction. It certainly could not generate enough distance simply by bouncing off Fuqua's arm.*

THERE WERE A number of cameras, some from the NFL, some from NBC. They were in different locations, and that was important. It depends on which angle you are looking at. On one, you are seeing the event from the side. On another, you are seeing it from the end zone. There are a couple where the cameras are down low and at least one where the camera is up pretty high. If you can see all of those, you get a very good idea of what was going on. Anybody can see it, especially if you do some calculations. It's clear. There's no option. The answer is that the ball ricocheted after hitting Tatum. This is not an opinion, it is a measurement.

Hank Gola. In 1997, the twenty-fifth anniversary of the Immaculate Reception, he was the first person—he was a sportswriter at the *New York Daily News*—to call me up, in 1997, and he said he had a clip of the play and wondered if I could do something using science and mathematics, could I come to a definite result. That's what started my interest into this, into applying physics to this play. What I did to simulate this was to use a football and throw it at a brick wall. I measured the velocity of the rebound and how far it rebounded, and I could not get it anywhere close on the rebound compared to what the rebound was off of Tatum. Bradshaw's pass, in order to rebound as far as it did (27 feet) to reach Franco Harris, had to rebound at 30 feet/second. That is what it was in the game.

The films made it easy to measure distances and times that, with the help of Isaac Newton's laws of motion and gravity, led to the answer of the question of whether the ball hit Tatum. The important facts I found from that film are those labeled A, B, C, and D, below. The result labeled E was obtained from measurements taken while bouncing the football against a brick wall.

A. Tatum was running very fast upfield (i.e., toward the ball) when the ball hit.
B. Fuqua had no velocity component upfield when the ball hit.
C. Bradshaw's pass was moving downfield with a speed of 64 feet/second when it hit either Fuqua or Tatum.
D. When Bradshaw's pass rebounded from the football player, it was moving at 30 feet/second.
E. When a football hits a brick wall at 64 feet/second, it rebounds at most 14 feet/second.

The logic is straightforward: It's obvious that a ball hitting a brick wall will rebound faster than if it had hit a stationary person. If Bradshaw's pass (point C) had hit Fuqua (points B and E), the ball would have rebounded slower than 14 feet/second (point E) and could not have gone far enough to reach Harris. The rebound on the field went at a speed of 30 feet/second (point D). Therefore the ball couldn't have hit Fuqua. It had to have rebounded from a person moving fast upfield—in other words, Tatum.

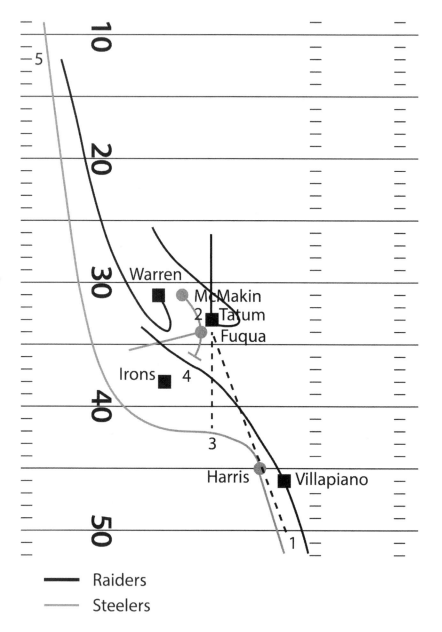

Source: Froggy88 via Wikimedia Commons

CHAPTER 4

SUPER BOWL IX: BREAKING THROUGH

	1	2	3	4	OT	Final
Steelers	0	2	7	7		16
Vikings	0	0	0	6		6

It is easy, through the haze of decades, to tie together the Immaculate Reception and the outset of the Steelers' 1970s dynasty. But it didn't quite work that way. First, the Steelers followed their thrilling win over the Raiders with the 1972 conference championship game in Pittsburgh (the location of the game alternated between divisions each year) against the undefeated Dolphins. There, on a flukishly warm New Year's Eve—it was around 60 degrees in Pittsburgh, erasing the Steelers' cold-weather advantage over Miami—Pittsburgh fans watched as Terry Bradshaw was knocked out of the game with a concussion. He later returned, but not until after the 10-7 halftime lead was erased and turned into a 21-10 deficit. Bradshaw gamely brought the Steelers back but ran out of time, and Miami kept its unbeaten year alive with a 21-17 win.

The momentum-changer in the game, though, came thanks to a second-quarter fake called by punter Larry Seiple, who had once converted a fourth-and-41 for a 70-yard touchdown while in college at Kentucky. This one didn't go for a touchdown, but it did go for 37 yards, as the Steelers didn't seem to recognize Seiple's ploy until he'd already gone 20 or 25 yards. That set up Miami's first touchdown, after the Steelers defense had throttled the Dolphins. And Miami didn't stop tormenting the Steelers the following year, either. The 1973 season was rough going for the Steelers, who finished 10-4 despite a shoulder injury to Bradshaw that forced backup Terry Hanratty into four starts. There was also a start that season for star-crossed third-string quarterback Joe Gilliam, who opened a Monday night game against the Dolphins on December 3, 1973, by going 0-for-7 and throwing three interceptions. The Steelers fell behind, 30-3, and a tender-shouldered Bradshaw was pressed into action. He, too, threw three interceptions but did rally Pittsburgh back to 30-24 before Miami ended the game by taking a safety to make the final 30-26. The Steelers made the 1973 playoffs but were dispatched by the Raiders, 33-14.

Dick Anderson

Defensive Back

Team: *Miami Dolphins, 1968-77*

Dick Anderson was part of the undefeated 1972 Dolphins that stopped the Steelers after the Immaculate Reception and played a significant role in the 1973 Monday night defeat in Miami that was a key part of the unraveling of the Steelers late in the season. Anderson returned an interception for a touchdown against Joe Gilliam, then picked off Bradshaw three times, including once for a touchdown, for four interceptions.

PEOPLE SAID WE had a lack of emotion (in 1972). We went about our preparation in a very businesslike manner. There wasn't a lot of rah-rah stuff. Today, teams with the best record would have the home-field advantage. We were undefeated and had won our division by the 10th game, so the last four games didn't mean diddly. But that was really to our advantage because, for one, we had to play an away game when we had a perfect season. Second, what was fortuitous was it was 60 degrees that day in Pittsburgh.

Our punter, Larry Seipel, won the game for us. He's back to punt and we're on our 40, and he went up to Shula and said, 'I think we ought to be able to do a fake punt because they're getting into our wall pretty quick.' Shula just looked at him and said, 'If you're going to do it, you better make it. Just don't screw up.' In the highlight film he's just running down the field and he's running right behind the Steelers. Larry was a tight end and he was an athlete. They're running down the field toward the ball, and he's just running along right behind them.

We were able to hold down their running game. We paid special attention to making sure the play went inside instead of outside. Franco was more of an outside back because he'd bounce out a lot. So we prepared and worked to keep runners in the middle. The off guard told me 100 percent of the time where he was going. I remember one time Franco either broke through the line or caught a little swing pass. It was just he and I in the open field. He hit me pretty good, but I was able to tackle him. It was one of the few times that Shula congratulated me for a play.

Franco was a marvelous player. He was just a big strong fullback who could cut going full speed. Anybody who is bigger than you, and running at you, and has an angle, is going to be hard to tackle. I tackled with my shoulder and my head. I was kind of an old-style tackler and would get my head in front. But you get a big guy like that and he was going to whack you. Franco was a very athletic, big, fast guy. With Franco, you knew you were going to get hit if he was coming at you. So I always tried to have an angle so he couldn't hit me head-on.

(In terms of the 1973 Monday night game) in general you're never going to get four interceptions in a half as a team anyway, it just so happened that I had them all. I was the leading receiver in yards, catches, touchdowns, and points. I told Terry that one time on his TV show, when he was talking to Larry Csonka, Jim Kiick, and myself. I mentioned that to Terry, I said, 'I really appreciate being your main receiver that night.' He didn't think it was quite as funny as I did. It was just one of those nights when the stars were aligned. The defense was called and I reacted. And I should have had a third touchdown, on the third one I got pulled down on the 1-yard line. If I would have zigged instead of zagged, I would have had three touchdowns. And, I would have had a fifth interception in the fourth quarter but I jumped and my legs cramped and a ball Bradshaw threw went right over my fingertips. God decided I wasn't going to have the record.

Each quarterback had to make the read on the snap because they couldn't figure out what we were doing. Whether it was a blitz or man coverage or a zone, we lined up the same distance, same place, and same formation every time. After Gilliam threw the two inter-ceptions, they put Bradshaw in and he hadn't played for a while. When he came in in the first half he was a little rusty, and I don't think he expected to play, so that could have helped me get those interceptions. And in the second half, I think we were probably easing up a little bit and they were pissed off and coming after us. They came out in the second half with more fire than we did and they started getting their act together. Bradshaw was warmed up and knew he was going to come in and they had confidence in that half. When they came out and scored all those points in the second half, it showed the potential they had. He was a great quarterback because the ball got there so damn fast. He could thread the needle and put it in there when other quarterbacks couldn't do that. I think Bradshaw was one of the first of that era who could really throw the ball like that.

His long passes were accurate and his short passes got there quicker. We hadn't seen arms like that. The great quarterbacks when I was a young player were just masters at knowing what to do, but then you get to the Bradshaws and the Marinos and that ball's really coming at you. Bradshaw would throw more passes into double coverage than Griese, because he could. He was certainly one of the great quarterbacks. What changed from the old quarterbacks to the Bradshaws and Marinos was, the ball got there a lot quicker. They were bigger and had great arm strength.

Bob Lilly

Like Anderson, Lilly was impressed by Bradshaw early in his career and had played against him in Dallas in Week 4 of the 1972 season, just Bradshaw's second full season as the starter. It was not an exceptional day for Bradshaw, who completed just 12 of his 39 passes for 166 yards in a 17-13 loss. But even then, both Lilly and Cowboys coach Tom Landry had a feeling about Bradshaw.

I DID PLAY AGAINST him once, early in his career, in the Cotton Bowl. For about a week before that game I had been bothered by a bone spur in my heel, which was very, very painful. So the doctor shot my ankle with Novocain before the game but he didn't put any deadening in it. When he gave me the shot I almost passed out. But we went out and played the game and I was lined up against this really quick, fast young guard. So I got loose and beat this kid and was going around him, and I had Bradshaw in my arms. This young guard clipped me from behind, and he clipped me right on my heel and it broke the bone spur off. I think Bradshaw slipped out of my hands. When I got up, I wanted to limp, but then I noticed my heel had quit hurting because the bone spur was gone. So Dr. Knight, our team doctor, he looked at it after and said, "I'll be darned. I got screwed out of a surgery this off-season."

I do remember thinking in that game that they were really going places. I recall that Bradshaw was very difficult to corner and catch and bring down. I had a grip on him two or three times in that game, but I never got my arms completely around him. He was very elusive. He had a sixth sense. He could be looking one way, but he felt the pressure coming. All the great quarterbacks that I've ever seen have that same aptitude to where they sense somebody coming from behind. Also that day I felt like he was a really good athlete. He was strong and he was quick. And his thought process was quick because he let go of the passes so fast. A lot of time a guy would hang on one last second and you could maybe hit him or get his arm or trap him. But I could see Bradshaw was going to be one of those guys who was tough to get. He wasn't Fran Tarkenton, who you would chase around scrambling all day, but he was a good scrambler. He knew how, at the last minute, how to get away. He was strong enough and a good enough athlete who could pull out of my arms. He was real young, of course, but I remember watching film and Coach Landry saying, 'This is an up-and-coming young quarterback.'

Ultimately, though, the new guys would need a year before their impact was felt. The 1974 Steelers were still very much Franco Harris's when it came to offense, as he racked up his second 1,000-yard season and the Steelers finished just 21st out of 26 teams in passing offense. Much of that stemmed from a lack of trust between Chuck Noll and Terry Bradshaw, who lost his starting job to Joe Gilliam early in the year and repeatedly was the subject of jokes about his intelligence. In the run-up to that year's Super Bowl, Bradshaw complained in a press conference, "I've been labeled 'Ozark Ike' and 'Dummy' and, 'Country Bumpkin,' and I hate it." But offensive turmoil almost didn't matter, because there was the defense: first in yards allowed, first in turnovers, second in points allowed. More important, they'd gotten better as the season went on, allowing just 9.0 points per game in the second half of the year. The defense was in peak shape when the playoffs came around.

In their playoff opener, the front four—the nascent Steel Curtain—of Joe Greene, Dwight White, L.C. Greenwood, and Ernie Holmes hammered Bills star running back O.J. Simpson, holding him to just 49 yards on 15 carries in a dominating 32-14 performance in Pittsburgh. In the conference championship, it was old friend Oakland and coach John Madden, who had drawn the ire of Chuck Noll when he dismissed the Steelers out-of-hand, saying of the Raiders' first-round matchup against Miami, "When the best plays the best, anything can happen." In Noll's pregame address to his players, linebacker Andy Russell reported that Noll said, "Well, they're not the best, and neither one of them's going to be in the Super Bowl." The Raiders gained just 29 yards rushing, and the Steelers picked off quarterback Ken Stabler three times as Pittsburgh won, 24-13. After the game, Madden conceded, "Their defense just crushed us."

It was thus that the Steelers went into the franchise's first championship game—Super Bowl IX—against a Minnesota team that also prided itself on its defense and had allowed only 24 points in two playoff games. On a slippery, chilly day in New Orleans, the Steelers' defense again carried the day against the Vikings, the two teams going into halftime with only a safety's worth of scoring and the Steelers holding a 2-0 lead. Pittsburgh limited Vikings great Chuck Foreman to a measly 18 yards on 12 carries and sealed the game on defensive back Mike Wagner's interception. The final was 16-6, Minnesota getting its only points on a blocked punt recovered in the end zone. Considering how long a wait it had been, Bradshaw—sometimes maligned by fans and media in the previous two seasons—gave a nod to his biggest backer, the Chief. "Winning this game for Mr. Rooney was the big thing," he told reporters.

Paul Krause

Defensive Back/Wide Receiver

Teams: Washington Redskins, 1964-67; Minnesota Vikings, 1968-79

The Vikings were making their third appearance in the Super Bowl when they faced the Steelers, and they'd lost their first two. They'd established one of the NFL's great defenses, with an imposing line of their own—the Purple People Eaters—and would, of course, go to four total Super Bowls from 1969 to 1976 without winning one. But star defensive back Paul Krause, a Hall of Famer who recovered a fumble in Super Bowl IX, never felt bitterness over that.

I **WAS DRAFTED BY** the Redskins, but Otto Graham traded me after a couple of years. I never really knew why, I just didn't think that was a good decision by him. But it was good for me to go to the Vikings, it all worked out. Bud Grant was a great coach and he had a lot of guys on that team who could make big plays. We had really great athletes who were also game-changers, we were aggressive and our coaches wanted us to be aggressive. We were a close team, we were really like a family, a lot like the Steelers. We had some great players up front and we had a lot of very good role players. Even in the Super Bowl games we lost, we always had good chemistry with each other. I think you could say we should have won one of the Super Bowls. We were good enough. But that's just how football goes sometimes, it's history now. When we went against Pittsburgh, it was 2-0 at halftime, and we just knew it was going to be that kind of game, defensive. That was our strength and their strength. But they just had a really great defense there, and they got enough of the breaks to win.

Ed White

Ed White entered the league in the same draft class as Joe Greene but was chosen by Minnesota. Playing in different conferences, the two did not match up very often until White left for San Diego in a trade in 1978 (he was a Charger until 1985). But when the Steelers did go up against the Vikings in Super Bowl IX, Pittsburgh's deepest playoff run to date, White was impressed by Greene's IQ for the game as well as his obviously physical skills, while also heaping praise on the play of the rest of the Steel Curtain defense. Pittsburgh—or, rather, Greene—was experimenting with a new adjustment in its 4-3 defense called a "tilted nose tackle," where Greene would line up between the guard and center, position himself at a 45-degree angle, then blast through the gap between the two linemen.

REMEMBER THE ANGLE and the stunt from Joe. Our defense was good, the Purple People Eaters. It was beneficial for us as an offense to practice against them. Joe Greene was really good, but so was Alan Page. It is so hard to pick out who was the best, because there are so many factors, but among the best I ever saw, Alan Page and Joe Greene would be right there. And Alan Page was someone I had to practice against every day. As an offensive lineman, that is how you make an offensive line. Alan was quicker, but Joe was more physical. They were different, but both were outstanding in those differences. The similarities were, anyone who is a great player is an intelligent player. They were both intelligent. If you've got brains as a defensive player, you've got a jump on things. There is just a sixth sense that some defensive linemen have, a gyroscope that just knows and goes in the direction of the ball. Because you're tuned in. It's all facilitated by your brain, which is this computer that has seen everything about this offense, this running back, this lineman, how he lines up, everything plugs into this sense. That was Joe Greene. As soon as your hat went a certain way, it just co-signed what he already knew and he was gone. And he was quick as a cat and big as a house.

But to me, it was a pretty close game going into the half and we fumbled the opening kickoff, Bill Brown fumbled the kickoff. They recovered it and went in and scored and the game was over after that. The tide turned. I think the first half was a pretty good battle. We didn't do much on offense, and they didn't either in the first half. It was a pretty good defensive battle. We continued not to do much in the second half, and they were able to start doing some things with the ball. It was a physical battle, and I think in terms of our passing game, we had a ton of passes swatted down. I think it was just a matter of, our quarterback was not a tall guy and you would be blocking their defensive front and all of a sudden a guy would jump up and bat the ball. I think L.C. Greenwood had three passes batted. That was an important part of their pass defense, timing it out at the line of scrimmage. It felt like that was the game plan.

I just think they had a better defense that day than we had offense. That day, they physically dominated us in the running game, and we just couldn't do much. From a linebacker standpoint, the Giants had a good group of linebackers at that time, and the Steelers were the other one. Those were the two best groups of linebackers. Think about that line, Joe Greene, Ernie Holmes, L.C. Greenwood, and Dwight White, that is a lot of defense there. They were champions, they deserved it.

SECTION 2

TRIUMPHS AND TRIBULATIONS

CHAPTER 5

SUPER BOWL X: DALLAS, PART I

	1	2	3	4	OT	Final
Steelers	7	0	0	14		21
Cowboys	7	3	0	7		17

The Steelers followed their win in Super Bowl IX with a masterpiece in 1975, a 12-2 season in which their only two losses came in Week 2 to Buffalo (O.J. Simpson gained 227 yards) and Week 14 in a meaningless game against the Rams in which Chuck Noll rested many of his top players. Most encouraging about the team's performance was the offense, which finally matched the outstanding defense that had carried Pittsburgh the previous year. During the 1974 season, even as they won the Super Bowl, quarterback Terry Bradshaw continued to be seen, in the eyes of most, as the team's weak link, with his intelligence the subject of repeated jokes and fans often calling for Terry Hanratty or Joe Gilliam to be the starter. Bradshaw turned the tables in 1975, earning his first Pro Bowl selection, throwing for 18 touchdowns against just nine interceptions, and establishing his career-best in quarterback rating, 88.0. Lynn Swann, too, earned a Pro Bowl berth, leading the league with 11 touchdown catches. The Steelers posted an average margin of victory of 15.1 points per game, a league best and a number that remains the highest in franchise history.

They won their first playoff game—the game that featured the introduction of the "terrible towels"—holding Baltimore to 10 points even with Joe Greene injured. Then it was the Steelers' most-hated rival, the Raiders, going up against Pittsburgh for the fourth straight year in the postseason. In the AFC Championship game, Greene made an inspiring return from injury, and the Steelers squeezed out a 16-10 win over the Raiders in a game that featured 13 turnovers, wind-chill temperatures below zero, and concussions suffered by Terry Bradshaw and Lynn Swann. The concussion for Swann, on a hit from George Atkinson, was especially severe, and he had to be taken to the hospital in an ambulance. Chuck Noll said it was the hardest-hitting game he had ever witnessed, and the *Pittsburgh Post-Gazette* noted that the Steelers-Raiders "hard-hitting series is starting to resemble the 30 Years War." But there was a bit of pregame controversy, too. Officially, the field at Three Rivers Stadium was slick with ice on the day of the game because of a torn tarp that left the sidelines of the field slicked with ice. That hurt the Raiders' passing game, as their perimeter receivers were left to slip and slide. The Raiders had questions as to how the field got so slick, however.

Mike Siani

Wide receiver

Teams: Oakland Raiders, 1972-77, Baltimore Colts, 1978-80

Mike Siani was a receiver in his fourth year with the Raiders when he faced the Steelers in the AFC Championship game, which was, amazingly enough, the seventh time the two teams had met from 1972 to 1975. Siani didn't find the slicked-up field to be an accident.

THEY TALK ABOUT Tom Brady and the air in the ball and all of that bull, but you don't know what cheating is until you walk into Three Rivers Stadium and it is 16 degrees below zero and they're hosing the field down with water, OK? Wait a minute, what's going on here? It's Astroturf, you don't need to water Astroturf. That was some pretty good cheating on their part. They got away with it. We showed up to play a football game but we are playing on a sheet of ice, because it's 16 below zero and the grounds crew is watering the field down.

Both teams were so talented that we always knew—when we got into training camp, one of the things John Madden would talk about when he stood in front of the team, even before the first practice, was, 'We gotta beat the Steelers.' We knew that every other team in the league, we were going to beat. We knew it. But he always said, 'if you want to get to the Super Bowl, we know the Steelers are going to be waiting for us, just like they knew we were going to be waiting for them at the end of the year.' Therefore, anytime we met during the season, which wasn't that often, we knew that we had to show them or they had to show us who was the dominant team. So things like Lynn Swann getting carried off the field on a gurney because he got clothes-lined by George Atkinson, or things like players yelling and screaming and calling each other names on the field, or taking cheap shots at guys, those were just things that happened because of the rivalry.

Having gotten by the Raiders, controversially (how else?), the Steelers had a surprise opponent in Super Bowl X—the rebuilt Dallas Cowboys, a team that coach Tom Landry had rejuvenated with help from a 1975 draft that had been nearly as productive as Pittsburgh's 1974 draft. The Cowboys had been a late-'60s powerhouse with their Doomsday Defense, but Landry was able to refurbish his roster so quickly that he now had a Doomsday Defense II on his hands. Dallas upset the hopes of the Vikings, seeking Super Bowl revenge on the Steelers, on a 50-yard Hail Mary pass from Roger Staubach to Drew Pearson in their playoff opener, then shocked the favored Rams with a blowout win in Los Angeles, 37-7, in the NFC Championship. That brought on the first installation of a bitter Cowboys-Steelers rivalry in Super Bowl X, at the Orange Bowl in Miami.

Charlie Waters
Defensive Back

Team: Dallas Cowboys, 1970-81

Waters and safety Cliff Harris made up what might have been the best safety combination in the league in the early 1970s, and one of the great combos of all time. They were hard-hitting against the run, adept in coverage, ardent studiers of film and—well ahead of their time—computer printouts. The cerebral nature of the Cowboys sometimes left them portrayed as softer than more traditional head-bangers like the Steelers, who were seen as brutes, which always bothered Waters.

THE 1975 GAME, we were a wild-card team and we got in, we sort of backed into the playoffs and they came back and beat us, it was a close game right down to the end. It was a defining moment for them, but also for us, it was the beginning of a four-year run for us, a new era, because we had 12 rookies make the team. We got a lot of players who were with us for a long time after that. It was the beginning of a nice run for us, there was the Doomsday Defense going back to the 1960s, but there was sort of the second version, we get this big draft—Randy White, Too Tall Jones—we put together an incredible defense, Doomsday II. We put together a run, we won one Super Bowl, we lost two to Pittsburgh, and lost once to the Rams in the playoffs. The Steelers were just a little ahead of us, in that 1975 Super Bowl, they had that much more experience and I think it showed in that game when they came back and beat us.

We were confident because we had momentum. It is a long NFL season, so finishing strong is a big thing, we always had that sign up in our locker room: Finish Strong. We finished strong and we carried that into the playoffs, so that was a big thing for us. One thing we did that was a little strange was we went back and watched old films of the Cowboys vs. the Steelers because we wanted to see how they blocked our flex defense from years before. The interesting angle on that, the brain trust—mostly Tom Landry, of course—felt that we should understand and study the times they played us in games and preseason games over the last five years or so. Instead of watching them play the last four or five games before the Super Bowl, we watched games they'd played against our flex defense before. Consequently, we were watching players who were not even on the team in 1975. I felt like that was a detriment to us as far as learning tendencies and studying personnel and figuring out how guys adapted, figuring out individual traits that certain players had. We missed all that, but we understood how they would block the flex defense, by golly. That was too simple. In a game, though, you learn a lot more, for me, by watching individual tendencies and seeing what kinds of things they give away.

When you watched the Steelers, you appreciated how simple their approach was. They were more just brute force, everybody going hard and knowing where they should be. The Cowboys defense was seen as more intellectual, and we were. Cliff and I, we had computer readouts, we were a little ahead of the rest of the NFL on that, studying tendencies through computer printouts we would memorize and know like the back of our hands. We had a reputation for being a little thoughtful, a little soft when it came to defense. I mean, I don't think anyone would tell you that Cliff Harris was not physical or Randy White was not physical or Ed Jones was not physical. But, we were thinkers, whereas the Steelers fought. They fought like hell. That was a big difference in philosophy and approach.

I think they had to pay attention to where we were, we would come up a lot—we had a lot of responsibility in defending the run, and you had to pay attention to where we were, we were basically running a 4-6 defense long before the Bears were doing it with Buddy Ryan.

Roger Staubach

Quarterback

Team: Dallas Cowboys, 1969-79

Offensively, there was no doubt where Dallas would be leaning in Super Bowl X—on its quarterback, Hall of Famer Roger Staubach, who earned his second Pro Bowl selection that year. But Staubach was short on weapons and found himself even shorter as the game progressed and the Cowboys lost some reliable receivers.

WE WENT INTO that Super Bowl with some confidence. We were a good team, but we did not have a strong running game, that was before Tony Dorsett. We had one really good wide receiver, Drew Pearson, and then some pretty good ones, like Golden Richards. But going up against the Steelers with their defensive backs, guys like Mel Blount and Mike Wagner, they were able to get up on top of the receivers. Drew, we had him in motion a lot, but we were kind of limited on offense. They shut down our running game, but we hit a couple of key passes that gave us a chance. But they were a better team that year, we were a wild-card team. Our defense played pretty darned good. I think we surprised them. We were big underdogs (seven points) in that game. It was a great Steelers team we lost to, and we were on the way to becoming the great team they were all through the 1970s. That '75 year was the beginning of us coming back, and we got Tony Dorsett in 1977, and that brought back our running game.

Our defense played well, and offensively, we hit a couple of touchdowns. I would say we played well on defense, and on offense, we struggled. I really did wish we had thrown the ball more in that game, and that had been the plan. We had some plays set up for our tight end, Jean Fugett, who was really taking advantage of the man-to-man defense and going inside on his release. He worked on it for two weeks, and we thought we could have an edge there. But he pulled a calf in the first quarter, so we did not have that there. But we were really planning on going more to the tight end because they were in man-to-man coverage and Jean could find some space in the middle.

Larry Cole

Defensive Lineman

Team: Dallas Cowboys, 1968-80

While Staubach and the Cowboys offense scraped for yards and points against Pittsburgh's tough front seven, the unique Cowboys defense—they ran what was called the 'flex' defense, with defensive tackles lining up off the line of scrimmage and each player required to read the offensive play as it was happening—was holding its own. Staubach started the scoring with a 29-yard touchdown in the first quarter on a crossing pattern to Drew Pearson, and Pittsburgh responded with a quick-strike touchdown a little more than four minutes later. From there, neither team scored in the first half, except for a Dallas field goal that put the Cowboys up at halftime, a lead they carried into the fourth quarter. Veteran defensive lineman Larry Cole was encouraged.

WE KNEW WE had a lot of good, young, talented guys. But this was the first year that Harvey Martin and Too Tall Jones had been starters. Bob Lilly had retired, I moved from end to tackle. Jethro Pugh was the only guy on that line who was a veteran playing his usual position. But we had a lot of good young bucks. We went into that game against the Steelers with a lot of young confidence, the older guys were sort of energized by these young bucks. It was all hopeful energy. The first play, we did a reverse on the kickoff and we started with the ball in their territory. Tom Landry obviously decided he was going for broke, and in a game like that, it was the right way to approach it. We were underdogs, but we let them know, we were in for the fight.

Landry did a great job of coaching that year. This was the first year Tom Landry put in the shotgun. No one was using the shotgun at that point. It was an old, old football thing, but at the time, Landry was the first to put it in and use it. It was a new thing. I remember against Los Angeles, when we beat the Rams, Fred Dryer and Jack Youngblood were the great ends on that team, and Landry put in these draw plays from the shotgun, and we'd hand it off and Preston Pearson would run right by those hard-rushing ends. We had wrinkles they had not seen before and that gave us a lot of confidence.

Our flex defense was different, it was difficult to explain. It was designed way back when to stop the Green Bay power attack. They would run power sweeps to the outside, and traps underneath, and power to the outside, and you knew that was what they were going to do, they were going to go back and forth. It was hard to stop, because if you lined up for one, they would run the other. So the flex was designed for that, it was a pretty complex defense. It wasn't very spontaneous, but if, at the end of the season, when everybody is focused in and everybody has been repeating it and knows what they're supposed to be doing, if everybody is doing their job, it was terrific to use and hard to block. Pittsburgh was not in our conference of course, so when they first saw our defense, I think they were kind of confused by it. Franco Harris, he had a lot of carries (27) but I don't think you'd say he had a lot of yards (82). We really shut them down pretty good in the run, and in the first half, third quarter, we were doing what we had to do to win the game.

Mel Renfro

Defensive Back

Team: *Dallas Cowboys, 1964-77*

The first thing that went wrong for the Cowboys was a special-teams breakdown in the fourth quarter, when punter Mitch Hoopes was lined up to kick from his own 16, tried to avoid a charging Reggie Harrison of the Steelers, but wound up having his punt blocked into the end zone for a safety to bring the Steelers within 10-9. That was especially deflating, because Hoopes kicked short on the punt that followed the safety, giving the Steelers good field position, which they eventually converted into a field goal and a 12-10 lead. Hall of Fame defensive back Mel Renfro could sense the frustration of yielding five points that way.

IT **WAS A** breakdown on the offensive line, that punt block. We were winning, 10-7. Mitch Hoopes was down near our goal line, their defense was really tough and there was a wind blowing so it was not going to be easy getting it out of there. Somebody screwed up and one of the Steelers (Reggie Harrison) came right through the middle of the line and blocked that punt out of the end zone, and so it was 10-9. For us, it was devastating because we knew if we were going to hold on and win the game, we had to do everything right, we were underdogs and you can't make mistakes in that position. We had them on the ropes, we had the game under control and we made a boo-boo, and it wound up biting us on the butt. We held them to just the field goal after that, but we went from having a lead to being behind pretty fast.

Charlie Waters

Another key for the Steelers in Super Bowl X: Lynn Swann had been hit hard by George Atkinson in the AFC Championship win over the Raiders, his head driven into the notoriously hard surface at Three Rivers Stadium. Swann had been knocked out and hospitalized, and there was some question as to whether he would play. When asked about Swann, Cliff Harris said, "I'm not going to hurt anyone intentionally. But getting hit again while he's running a pass route must be in the back of Swann's mind. I know it would be in the back of my mind." Swann said Harris's comments bothered him and added a little extra fire to his performance in Super Bowl X—though, as Harris would point out, he would have said the same about any receiver.

CLIFF CAME OUT in that 1975 Super Bowl, warning Swann not to go over the middle. Swann had gotten knocked out the game before against Oakland, and I think Cliff just wanted to keep that in the back of his mind. We figured he was going to play. But Swann took it as more of a challenge, like Cliff had provoked him. Cliff was not going to do anything dirty, he just played within the rules no matter who the receiver was. That was how Cliff was, he was going to hit you especially if you were coming over the middle, that was our responsibility. That was our job. But I think he got him going a little bit. It was not the type of attitude that Tom Landry coached us to be, he wanted us to lay low and not go making headlines. I think Cliff was really just saying that, hey, the guy could get hurt. But a lot of it was just media stuff. Cliff was a smart player and that was as important to him as anything he did physically.

I mean, Cliff used to hit players so hard, he would knock players out. I used to keep the stats every week, Cliff Harris's knockouts, how many wide receivers Cliff would knock out. He had a stretch where he knocked out eight in a row, they had to be carried off the field. So Cliff wasn't bragging about things, he meant he was going to hit Swann across the middle. But there was a lot more to his style of play than that. When there are two weeks before the game, and there is all this stuff going on, you say something and it sometimes gets rehashed over and over. You get caught up in the storm a little bit, that is how the Super Bowl is. You don't want to do that, and I don't think Cliff meant anything like he was going to try to hurt Swann. But things get blown up and maybe that got Swann fired up.

Cliff Harris

Defensive Back

Team: Dallas Cowboys, 1970-79

If there was a sense that the potential for a Harris-Swann confrontation had been blown out of proportion, that was confirmed once Super Bowl X got underway. For one thing, Swann did not typically run routes over the middle. And, as Harris points out, when Bradshaw looked for Swann, he would typically throw the ball high, both to take advantage of Swann's leaping ability and to put Swann in less vulnerable positions— getting hit in the air, after all, takes away from a defensive back's ability to launch into a receiver and deliver a hard blow.

THERE WAS NEVER a time in those Super Bowls where Lynn Swann ran a route that could have been a collision route for me. He did not run a route that was—never ran a post route, never ran an in route, never ran a down-and-in. Never ran something that would give me the chance to hit him. Which was smart, you know? He did run the deep post, and that was the play where he ran a deep post when I was on a safety blitz, because they knew, it's a smart play. It's a basic, elementary, simple picking play that Terry probably could key. He could say, 'Hey, this is on a safety blitz, I can throw it as far down the field as I can and just let Lynn Swann go up and try to beat the cornerback.' One thing that Lynn Swann had was an incredible leaping ability, that he could have that spring in his legs. One of the things that made Lynn so hard was that he could catch an in route. What you usually see is when a quarterback throws an in route, he throws it right into the gut of the receiver. Throws it right into his hands and he gets ready to take the hit. It was a different way with Lynn Swann, they had a completely different approach with Swann and John Stallworth. What Terry would do is, if they ran a down-and-in-route, or an in route, he would throw it real high and they would leap up and try to outjump the corner or the safety. The collision therefore was not going to be as hard on Lynn in that sense, because you can't jump and hit a guy at the same time.

What you did with Lynn Swann was something different, and I realized that when I studied the films. Those in routes that Lynn Swann would run—he really didn't run those down-and-ins very often, he ran them out of play-action mostly—what Terry would do is just throw it up higher and Lynn would go up and catch it real high on those in routes. Those 'flips' sort of hits won't have the impact, you'll land on your back. It won't have the impact. You won't have the head-to-head. You might flip them, but what they'd do is tuck their legs and feet underneath them and take a fall in the air, and just land acrobatically. That's what it was, he was a great athlete in terms of things he would do in the air.

Mel Renfro

On one side, Renfro was assigned to handle John Stallworth and spent most of the game covering him. Stallworth had only two catches, one coming over the middle, where Renfro was not covering him, and one out in the flat, where Renfro closed quickly and made a tackle for a loss. But Swann was eager to take advantage of the Cowboys' other corner, Mark Washington, and did so with three remarkable circus catches—all of which took place with Washington in position for tight coverage. That includes a 32-yarder along the sideline that Swann came back for, leaping past Washington, in the first quarter, and the famed 53-yarder, when Swann again leaped over Washington, tapped the ball up, caught it as he fell, and got up to run until Renfro came over to make the tackle.

LYNN SWANN HAD gotten hit pretty hard in the AFC (Championship) and some people said maybe he would not play, but we never thought that. We always thought he was going to play. Landry was that way about your opponents—never rule anything out. But if he was going to be out there, then we knew we had to control John Stallworth and Lynn Swann, and we spent a lot of time studying their tendencies. We thought Swann would play, but we were going to be ready one way or the other. They were going to get up the field and they were going to try to make plays to those guys. Unfortunately, Mark Washington just did not have a very good game. I remember one occasion, he got beat on a pass, Swann beat him. He was right there but that was the play where Swann just went up and grabbed the ball and kind of kept his focus and made the play. I was covering Stallworth, but I looked over and Swann had the ball, so I had to run all the way across the field to make the tackle on Swann, keep him out of the end zone. I read in the paper the next day, it said, 'Renfro got beat on the play.' I said, 'Boy, I tell you, sometimes the guys in the press box do not know what is going on on the field.'

Mark was a great cover guy. But he couldn't finish. He would stay with his guy, he would be on top of his guy, he was good with that. But he couldn't finish, and he got a reputation for that and he lost his position because of it. Great mobility, could backpedal, could cover. But he could not finish the play, and it was not just in that one game against Swann. That hurt him over and over. Mark was getting beat up in that game, and there was no way we could cover for him, he was mostly on Swann one-on-one on his own. I was covering Stallworth in that game, that was my job. He barely caught a pass. He caught one pass inside, over the middle, that was not my responsibility—my coverage was short outside, deep outside, and maybe the post play. The one pass Stallworth did catch, Terry threw it to him in the flat area and I made the play, he lost yards. I had a great day, and I felt great about the way our defense played that day. They were the mighty Steelers and we battled them right down to the final play.

Larry Cole

Despite their fourth-quarter foibles, the Cowboys had kept the Steelers from pulling away, and Pittsburgh was ahead only by a 15-10 margin with 3:31 to play when Bradshaw lined them up for a third-and-4 play at their own 36-yard line. Needing a stop, the Cowboys called for a blitz—and they nearly wrangled Bradshaw for a loss on the play, Larry Cole arriving with the hit just as Bradshaw was releasing the ball. Bradshaw managed to fire a pass to Swann, who capped his 161-yard day with a 64-yard touchdown catch, again just over the hand of Mark Washington. Pittsburgh led, 21-10.

WE HAD A blitz on and Cliff Harris went first, it was a safety blitz, and I hit Terry right after—today, I'd get fined for it because it was helmet-to-helmet contact, hitting him. But the thought was that if I could have done it half a second earlier, I would have disrupted the pass or sacked him. That would have made a big difference. We had the lead, and we were losing momentum and a lot of things happened. But the Swann touchdown kept things going in their favor.

If I had been there just a little earlier, that play does not happen and maybe Terry goes out of the game, they would have to get their backup in. Then we might have won the game. It was one of those things where Terry knew he was going to get hit but he hung in there strong and took the hit but got the pass off. That's what he always did so well, he was not worried about getting hit, he would take the contact but he was going to make his throw and then you could take your shot. But he had a good sense about making that throw. That's what he did there. That was basically the dagger.

It was a safety blitz, so basically my job in that situation is to make contact with the guard, then let the lane open up for him to blitz, throw off my block and follow him. Cliff got rolled out, he got bumped by the blocker a little bit and when he started going for Cliff, I threw him off and started going for Terry. Cliff and I were both there. Not only did he throw the pass before I could get there, it was a perfect throw that Swann caught in full stride. I did not see him catch it, but you could see the reaction down the field. Terry was on the ground, he'd gotten hit pretty hard, and Cliff and I were standing there and you can see what's going on downfield and we just dropped our heads and said, 'Sh–.' It was a pretty big play. It was third down, it was in their territory, it was late in the fourth quarter and we thought we were getting the ball back, you know, down by five. That was really crucial. If we got the ball back, our offense could have shown some life there.

Cliff Harris

The call for Harris to blitz on the critical pass to Swann came from the sideline; and though D.D. Lewis, Harris, and Cole all came close to laying a hit on Bradshaw, he was able to get the throw off.

LYNN HAD HIS best performance when I was on a safety blitz and Terry would just blindly throw it down the middle of the field and that's when Lynn made that leaping catch in the middle. I wish that I had not been on a safety blitz, I'd have been in the middle and that would not have been a complete pass, because I would have stopped it. It was one of those passes that demanded a hit. That was a long, deep pass that depended on pass defense, and I don't even think Terry would have thrown it had I been playing free safety because he would know I would have gotten it. But it was smart in a very basic, elementary thought process—hey, if the free safety is not in the middle, throw it down the middle. I am sure Chuck Noll said, Terry, here's the key, if you don't see Cliff Harris in the middle, throw it long deep because he could outleap the other guys. But don't throw it down the middle if Cliff is there.

Blaine Nye

Offensive Lineman

Team: Dallas Cowboys, 1968-76

Blaine Nye was a Pro Bowl right guard in 1974, and a founding member of the "Zero Club," the group of Cowboys linemen who did their best to avoid publicity.

I REMEMBER A BIT about it, most of it bitter. That was the year of Pat Donovan and Ed Jones, there was a whole bunch of them. It was a good rookie year. I think we expected to win it, I think we expected a good game. What I do remember most is that play to Lynn Swann, when he had the catch over Mark Washington, right over his fingertips. That was the kind of play that turned a game like that, one of those games where you have it won except for the breaks. It was going to be give-and-take, and we were throwing for the end zone at the end. Pittsburgh was a tough team but we were not terrified of them, we had come back from other deficits before. It was tough and they were physical, but at that point it was not yet a rivalry—it wasn't like my high school team, where we would get into fights after every game against our rivals.

Mel Renfro

It was only two games earlier that the Cowboys pulled off their Hail Mary comeback against the Vikings, and even down, 21-10, with a little more than three minutes to play, all was not lost. The Cowboys began to push furiously for a comeback.

WHEN YOU ARE playing for Coach Landry, there is always optimism. We felt good about our ability to play against the Vikings, we felt like we had that game under control. For some reason, we were behind at the end of that game, and fortunately, Roger Staubach threw the Hail Mary to Drew Pearson and we managed to win that one. But we thought we could win that game all along. That last drive, sure, we had our fingers crossed. We thought we had a chance, and we knew what Roger was capable of. We saw it in Minnesota. We didn't think we were going to win that game in Minnesota at the end, but we did and that gave us confidence that maybe it could happen again.

Roger Staubach

Staubach did give the Cowboys one last gasp of life. Using just a little more than a minute, Staubach drove the Cowboys within striking distance of the end zone and finished the drive with a 34-yard touchdown to Percy Howard, an undrafted rookie signee. The Cowboys defense held Pittsburgh to a 4-and-out on the ensuing drive, and Staubach moved Dallas to the Steeler 38 with 1:06 to play. Staubach could not complete another pass, though, and his final throw was picked off by Glen Edwards in the end zone, locking up a 21-17 Steeler win.

WE HAD A receiver there, Percy Howard, a very good athlete, who caught a pass for a touchdown in that game, and it was his only catch as a Cowboy in his career. He had an injury and never caught another pass for us, just one Super Bowl touchdown. Again, we had been dealing with injuries the whole game.

We had opportunities, too. And we gave them opportunities. I had a couple of interceptions that, because of our defense, they were not able to do much with. The turnovers were a problem, but still, we had a chance to win against one of the great Steelers teams, and we just didn't. I think we overachieved in that game, and they might have felt like they had it made going into that game, but we played a pretty good game. We got the ball back at the end, and hit a couple passes. But the clock was working against us. The last play, we were in position, and we were hoping for another Hail Mary. But it was Edwards, the safety, who got a hand on it and it was an interception, and that's how it ended. If we make that play, we could have won. It was down to the last play. It was a better game than people expected.

Cliff Harris

All in all, Harris had been given the bad-guy image in Super Bowl X, but it was one that was largely undeserved. His comments about Swann had been matter-of-fact, and his patting the head of kicker Roy Gerela after a missed field goal—to which Jack Lambert took offense and slammed Harris for—was an instinctual reaction that he says he'd take back if he could. Maybe the Steelers derived some emotional fire from Harris, but in reality, in a Super Bowl, emotions will run high no matter what is said.

I THINK I WAS miscast in all that villain mentality, particularly in that Super Bowl because throughout my career, I did not go around telling people, I am a tough safety, I'm a real hitter. I never did that. I did talk through my actions. But I wasn't one of those guys who was always trying to be tough. I was a guy that was doing a job, and part of my job was the physical side of it, and I was going to do what I could with it. I think what happened in that Super Bowl was, just through the press, it magnified my physical nature to a larger extent than it really was. My mental side was just as critical as my physical side. Jack Lambert was known as a tough guy, no teeth, all of that. I was tough, and I knocked guys out, but I was also a smart guy that beat guys strategically. The press took that away in that Super Bowl.

The thing about it is, you've got to remember, when you're playing in a Super Bowl, if you're not hyped up and ready to play in a Super Bowl, then you're probably not going to be in a Super Bowl. The defense of Pittsburgh was not going to get even more hyped up than they always were because of something I did.

CHAPTER 6

"THE BEST STEELER TEAM OF ALL TIME"

AFTER THEIR SECOND straight Super Bowl and with the bulk of their starters all in their early-to-mid 20s, Pittsburgh appeared set up for a long run of Super Bowl championships in the mid-70s. However, 1976 didn't get off to a great start, beginning with the opener in Oakland, in which a Franco Harris fumble in the fourth quarter of a game the Steelers led, 28-14, opened the way for a surreal finish, the Raiders scoring 17 points in the final three minutes to win, 31-28. In the game, Lynn Swann—away from the play at the time—took a cheap shot to the back of the head from defensive back George Atkinson, and after the game, Noll lamented the presence of a "criminal element" in the NFL. Charging defamation, Atkinson sued Noll and the Steelers for $3 million.

On the field, things didn't improve. Pittsburgh began the year 1-4, including a home loss to the Patriots and road losses to Minnesota and Cleveland. The loss to the Browns was especially disheartening, because Terry Bradshaw had to be carried off on a stretcher after a vicious body slam from Browns defensive end Turkey Jones, and the Steelers were planted in last place in their division. "We're about as good as Holy Trinity Grade School right now," said a furious Noll after the Cleveland game. But a strange thing happened with Bradshaw out, and even after he returned still not quite 100 percent healthy. The Steelers defense started to pick up the slack for its missing quarterback. They allowed just six points in Week 5. They put together three consecutive shutouts in midseason and closed the year with two more shutouts. After their dreadful start, the Steelers rallied to win nine straight—allowing only 28 points, or 3.1 points per game, in those nine games—and finish first in their division again, earning a return trip to the playoffs.

Steve Grogan

Quarterback

Team: New England Patriots, 1975-90

Steve Grogan was the quarterback of the Patriots in 1976, his first full year as a starter. The Patriots had been 3-11 the previous season, so going into Three Rivers and coming out with a 30-27 win that was capped by a bootleg-run touchdown was a monumental confidence boost for a team that went on to a huge turnaround, an 11-3 record, and might have seen the Steelers later in the year in the postseason, if not for a controversial roughing the passer call that cost New England a sure win in their playoff game against the Raiders.

WHEN I WENT to college (at Kansas), the Steelers was the team you watched. They were the best. I would watch Terry Bradshaw and I wanted to do the things he would do, I tried to copy some of those things—he was tough, he was a tough quarterback, he loved to throw the deep ball and take those chances down the field. We had the same thing, I loved the way he played the game. Then suddenly, you are on the same field as them. Their fans were rabid because of the two Super Bowl wins by the time I came around. It was an intimidating place to play in, the ground was hard, but the toughest thing was, they had guys on both sides of the ball that were going to be Hall of Famers. So you had to play a great game if you even wanted to have a chance.

It was my first year as a starter. We had started the season off pretty well after a poor 1975 season. We went to Pittsburgh, and it was a back-and-forth game, but we wound up on top. It was a huge win for a young team at that time. I remember running one in, the one that we wound up winning on, and I had to give a stiff-arm to Joe Greene for that. I remember Russ Francis, our tight end, taking one down the sideline about 40 yards for a score. A lot of things fell into place that were big for us.

There was a point, and it was late in the game, and I fumbled the ball and I was diving to get it back. Of course, you wind up in a big pile, there are guys falling on you all around. I remember getting up and I turned around and bumped into L.C. Greenwood sort of after the play was over. I ran into him and Greenwood, I remember him spitting at me. Right at me, it was no accident. I was a young guy but I did not want to look like I was intimidated so I went to spit back at him. But I had cottonmouth. I couldn't get anything out to spit back at him. I was too nervous. I was planning on being tough but it just didn't happen.

There was another play with Jack Lambert. They would, a lot of the time, play their defense with their tackles spread out really wide. That would leave Lambert lined up six yards deep in the middle of the field. We put in the play called the 'Goose' play, and basically, it was a surprise play, I would just pinch the center to signal it and, because I was a good runner, the center would just go forward and I would follow him, he would block Lambert and we'd get a good gain. We were backed up on our 5-yard line, we were deep in our territory. They spread the tackles, so I called the Goose play, and we ran it and I got a first down out of it. Next play, we get up to the line of scrimmage and Lambert was not back in the middle, he was up at the line, almost leaning all the way over the center. He looks me in the eye, right across from my face, and says, 'If you do that play again, you blankety-blank, I am going to rip your head off!' That was my wake-up call, welcome to the NFL. They didn't play that defense again, so I didn't have to try the play again. But he was a little bit intimidating, wasn't he?

We won that game, but they were the best defense I ever saw. I played against them and I played against the 1985 Bears in the Super Bowl, unfortunately. I would put them both up there at the top all-time.

Mike Siani

Jack Lambert had earned his first Pro Bowl selection in 1975, his second season, but he was even better in 1976, leading the league with eight fumble recoveries and being chosen, for the first time, as a first-team All-Pro. He intimidated receivers against coming over the middle, and Siani said he could accomplish that just with his demeanor and looks.

COMPARE HIM TO Dick Butkus. When he hit you, he not only hit you, he didn't want you to get back up. So if you caught a ball and he tackled you, he then tried to keep you on the ground. He would push you back down, step on you, step on your chest. He would tell you in uncertain terms, 'Don't ever come over the middle again.' I hope I never see him again, because he'll tear my head off. But he looked like an orangutan on the field. You know how he was built, so when he would get down into his football position at the linebacker position, his knuckles were scraping on the ground, his wingspan was something like eight feet, and he looked like an orangutan.

John Banaszak

Team: *Pittsburgh Steelers, 1975-81*

John Banaszak was an undrafted free agent from Eastern Michigan in 1975, and of all the teams on which to find a spot for an undersize defensive end, the Steelers figured to be the toughest. But learning to play a role in order to land on the roster of the 1975 team gave him entry into the NFL, and practicing with and against the Steelers of the mid-to-late-1970s taught him enough to keep him in the league for seven seasons. In 1976, injuries forced Banaszak (now head coach at Robert Morris) and others into action—and they universally responded.

FOR ME, IT was a great experience going into camp, knowing it was a young team and, obviously, the odds were not in my favor. But George Perles laid it all out for us the first meeting we had in camp in Latrobe. He told us, 'There isn't anybody in this room who is going to beat out Joe Greene or Ernie Holmes, Dwight White, or L.C. Greenwood, OK?' So he told us, the defensive linemen they were going to keep would be the ones who could make a contribution on special teams and I felt that was the door that opened up for me at that time. They cut the rosters from 48 to 43 that year, so that made things a little tougher. But once I heard George Perles say that about special teams, I thought I had a chance, because I was undersize for the line, I was 230 pounds, but I could run.

In 1976, I made my first start against the Giants. Dwight and Ernie were both hurt, so Steve Furness and I made quite a few starts in the middle of the year. It was a great defensive effort that year, after we were 1-4. We were two-time defending champions and Bradshaw got dumped on his head in Cleveland and was out. I knew I was surrounded by great players and that took a lot of pressure off me.

I was playing alongside Joe Greene, and you have Greenwood on the other side, Andy Russell, Jack Ham, and Jack Lambert behind you. That gives you room to make a mistake and know that your teammates are going to be there to help you out. My goal at that point was to, similar to what Chuck taught us, you play with your fundamentals and stick with that. I spent a lot of time my rookie year watching Joe and Ernie and all of those guys, studying film so I could figure out how to play as much like them as I possibly could.

The pass rush techniques that L.C. Greenwood had, those techniques were ones that—he was so fluid and so long that there was no way I could do the same things he could do. But Dwight, I could learn a lot from Dwight because we were the same physically. I knew that Dwight played with an awful lot of toughness, he was physical in the way he attacked. That pretty much was something that I could do, I figured. So I learned a lot from him about playing defensive end. I was not going to play like Joe Greene, but I could play with the intensity Ernie Holmes had. I could play with the intensity of Dwight White and Steve Furness. I still have video of one-on-one pass rushes from those days that I put on for my kids. It was almost vicious, the practices we had, the one-on-ones. You never wanted to have a bad rep, all the time. In some ways, the practices were a lot harder than the games. That was something I always took from that group of guys. You have an opportunity to be good, but if you work hard, you could fit in to what they were doing there.

We were 1-4, our backs were against the wall. We had a bunch of injuries, Swann was out, Ernie and Dwight White were both out, but without Bradshaw, our defense was under that much more pressure. (Backup quarterback) Mike Kruczek threw 10 passes per game, that was what we needed from him. His arm was not sore, that is for sure. He had to turn around and hand it to Franco and Rocky, two legitimate 1,000-yard rushers and two guys who really brought up their game when we had those injuries. They were in a situation where the defense knew they were going to run the football, but they did it anyway.

It was amazing. The defense knew, first and second down, we were running the ball. They were stacking eight, nine people in the box, but our offensive line still moved the ball, controlled the clock, we didn't turn the ball over.

We knew we were not going to score that many points, and we had to win by running the ball and playing great defense. We put together a streak of great defense that I don't think the NFL has seen since. You can take the 1985 Chicago Bears and talk about them all you want, but what we did in 1976 was absolutely amazing, the shutouts, giving up 28 points in nine ballgames, it was incredible. We were a desperate football team that could not afford to lose another game and went out every week with the intention of shutting down the offense.

The Chief (Art Rooney) said it best when he said that was the best Steeler team of all time.

Given the unusual route the Steelers took to the playoffs in 1976, it should have come as little surprise that their postseason was equally bizarre. Pittsburgh played their postseason opener in Baltimore and drubbed the Colts, 40-14, behind 132 yards from Franco Harris, in one of the most lopsided playoff games in league history. It turned out that the blowout was a stroke of good fortune, because it meant that most fans in the upper deck cleared out well before the game's end. About 10 minutes after the game officially was over, a mentally unstable, recently laid-off amateur pilot buzzed Baltimore's Memorial Stadium in a small rented plane, touching down on the field before pulling up—but not in time. The plane crashed into the upper deck. No one, including the pilot, was seriously injured. Given all that the team had gone through in 1976, when the Steelers went on to lose to the Raiders in the AFC Championship the following week, it was almost anticlimactic.

John Dutton

Defensive Lineman

Team: Baltimore Colts, 1974-78; Dallas Cowboys, 1979-87

Dutton was a standout defensive end in 1976, when he made his second consecutive Pro Bowl for Baltimore. The Colts had been one of the top defensive teams in the league and ranked seventh in stopping the run. But the simple, well-executed plays for Harris, John Fuqua, and Reggie Harrison just proved to be too much for Baltimore, which allowed 225 yards rushing, then saw their stadium serve as the site of a bizarre crash-landing.

THEY DIDN'T DO a whole lot, they just did everything so well. I know we tried to stop the running game with Bleier and Franco, and they had certain plays they would run, almost like a little counter play and we just couldn't stop the play very well. That running play, you didn't know if they were going to hand it off to Rocky or Franco, but the guard would pull and if you thought it was going to be a trap, then it wasn't a trap, it was an outside play, or they could turn it inside. They did it so well, they could switch up on that play, give it to Franco or Rocky, and there was no indication which way it was going, so you were just guessing all the time. They just needed somebody to not be doing their job and they would break you. They kept running that damn play the whole game. If you started to focus on that, though, then they've got Bradshaw and the two receivers going downfield, and you have to cover them, too. It's the kiss of death.

We had a good defense, we played well all year. But Franco had a really good game against us. We had a good front four and our linebackers were serviceable. But they were one of those teams that could just run their plays like they were in practice, run their plays and you might know it is coming but they were just so good at what they did. And that offensive line never gets enough credit. They were very strong and such great pass blockers. I played against Jon Kolb and he was an excellent, excellent blocker, he had great feet and strong as a bull. He could just punch you out and you're there trying to get around him, but he wasn't going to let you. Even on the plays you did, Bradshaw was such a tough guy to deal with, he was not going to be an easy guy to bring down.

It seemed like every time we played them while I was with Baltimore, that was how it went. They just came out and executed their plays really, really well. We had the better record, we were thinking maybe we would be able to get that deal done, but it just didn't happen. I always enjoyed playing against those guys, because they were so good at what they did. It wasn't enjoyable playing them, but it was enjoyable in that if you could do something with them, you knew you accomplished something.

After the game, I had no idea about the plane crash at first. At that time, my wife, Ginny, and Bert Jones's wife were walking from the press box down to where our locker room was, with my agent, Howard Slusher. They were in the bathroom and Howard saw the plane and had no idea what was happening, so he ran into the bathroom and started screaming to them that a plane had crashed into the end zone. We were down there, right below that, and we don't even hear it. That stadium was like pure concrete. But someone told us and we went up and we're looking and there it is, an airplane stuck straight up in the end zone seats. It was one of those days, you know? A fitting ending for us. A crash.

John Banaszak

Banaszak was in his second NFL season in 1976 and said the Steelers were comfortably in their locker room when the plane crashed into

Baltimore's Memorial Stadium. But as video of the incident rolled on the television sets behind Chuck Noll, players were more than a little distracted.

THIS CLOWN APPARENTLY tried to do a touch-and-go, right at the end of the game. We clobbered the Colts pretty well, and we were all in the locker room. Chuck is talking to us, we just got in the locker room, and they have three TV sets in the locker room, and they're all something like 18-inch screens, OK? It's not quite what we have today for televisions. Chuck is talking and the sound is down, but no one is paying attention to Chuck because there is a picture on the screen of a plane in the upper deck of Baltimore's stadium. On the bottom, there is a scroll and it says, 'Live from Baltimore.' Chuck's talking and everyone starts running out of the room to find out what the heck is going on. And sure enough, there is a plane sort of on its nose, crashed into the upper deck. The guy did a touch-and-go, he went in from the open end and did not have enough power to pull out of it in time. If the game had been closer, if there were people still sitting up there, there would have been some deaths. Fortunately, it was a blowout.

CHAPTER 7

AN UNRAVELING

FOR THE STEELERS, the 1977 season was a reflection of what had gone on in 1976. There was a disappointing loss to the Raiders early in the year and a 4-4 record at the eight-week mark, but unlike 1976, for this season, adversity did not yield a stronger bond—quite the opposite, in fact. The Atkinson lawsuit proved a major distraction, and while on the witness stand that spring, Noll conceded that some of his own players, including Joe Greene and Mel Blount, had been involved in dirty plays, too, and were part of the league's "criminal element." Blount was ticked off, and he threatened to sue Noll, too. Jack Lambert and defensive back Glen Edwards were upset about their contracts and threatened holdouts, with Lambert's agent saying he wanted to be traded. Making matters worse, Bradshaw suffered a broken wrist in the Steelers' second game and played hurt all year.

The Steelers won their division, but only because a 9-5 record was just enough to get past the rest of the sad-sack AFC Central. If they were to have a postseason rally, it would have to go through Denver, which finished 12-2 that year.

Tom Jackson

The Broncos had not made the playoffs in their 17-year history, but enjoyed a breakthrough year in 1977, led by the Orange Crush defense, which held opponents to a league-best 109.4 yards rushing per game. As a versatile linebacker, Jackson (now well known as an analyst for ESPN) earned the first of three straight Pro Bowl selections that year, playing alongside fellow Pro Bowl linebackers Lyle Alzado and Randy Gradishar. But it was when the Steelers showed up in Denver for the opener of the 1977 playoffs that Jackson—with two key interceptions and a fumble recovery—shone brightest. The final score was 34-21, but the game itself was much closer than that, at least until Jackson stepped in.

BY THAT TIME, we had developed into a good team. My rookie class was a class where they finally started to have some success. Paul Howard, Calvin Jones, Barney Chavous came in and was on the defensive All-Rookie team. We started having some success and there was a core of players there, at least a few, who we could build around. We had Louis Wright, Rubin Carter was the best nose tackle in the game. Lyle Alzado was there. We were playing a 3-4 scheme at that time which was a little unusual then, I know everyone plays some version of it now. We had the Orange Crush defense, some very capable players offensively. It was like, if the offense could hold its own, we would be able to, as a defense, win us the game. We got Craig Morton, he was a veteran. They have this term now, game-manager, and I think even at that time, Craig was that kind of guy. He was able to manage an offense that was built to complement a great defensive team.

We knew the kind of defense we had. But still, that Steelers defense would be, for my money, that would be the best defense I saw, ever. People will argue about 1985 Bears and different defenses along the way, the no-names of Miami, but the best I ever saw was Pittsburgh. We understood how good they were. We had beaten them in the regular season, and that was important for us. We gained confidence when we won games like that. We had the Raiders in our division, so we felt like those were the two teams everyone was focused on, and we were going up against them. In the AFC, if you were going to be the cream of the crop, you were going to have to beat Pittsburgh, you were going to have to beat Oakland. That was the measuring stick.

They had tied the game up in the fourth quarter, they obviously knew how to win, so we needed to make some plays that would give us momentum, and I was fortunate to be in position to do that with the two interceptions. Those plays, we talked a lot in our room with our defensive coordinator, Joe Collier, about game-changing plays. That is how we lived that season, we thrived on turnovers. In that game, too. The first interception was just a reflex play. It was right over the middle. I was not in man-to-man coverage, I was in kind of a zone and locked up with the back, who was still blocking. I would not try to remember the exact distance, but I was pretty close to the line of scrimmage. And Terry had an arm, he threw the ball hard. So I got my hand up and hit the pass, and it was a hard one, and it went straight up. At that point, all I had to do was bring it in. But it was pure reflex. The second one was just a flat route. It was one Terry probably wished he had back as soon as he threw it. He kind of threw the ball right at me, so it was easy, I just had to make the catch. But those plays set us up for scores, we needed that.

Funny thing about that game, my dad was in attendance for that game. A little extra motivation. I had a couple of interceptions, I had a fumble I got my hands on. At some point, I had the ball in my hands three times and set up a score. We felt like we were going to be competitive in that game. Defensively, we were a very challenging unit for anybody, even that team. And we knew how good they were. We firmly understood that this was a football team capable of greatness. I will tell you this, my dad was one of the more understated men you would ever meet in your life. After the game, I was getting dressed and I asked some friends if they would keep an eye on him while I was getting in the shower and getting ready to come out. In the area where they were tailgating after the game, my dad was there with some of my friends and I came out and got him, we got in the car. He turned to me and he said, 'Son, I want you to know, you played pretty well. You played a pretty good game.' If you knew my dad, you would know, that meant more to me than anything. That was my confetti ball, the confetti falling on me, for my dad to say I had a pretty good game.

Red Miller

Coach

Team: Denver Broncos, 1977-80

The 1977 playoff win over the Steelers was especially big for coach Red Miller, a career assistant who had taken over the head-coaching job from John Ralston that year. Miller eventually led the Broncos to the Super Bowl, but he'd long respected Chuck Noll as a coach, and the postseason win over Noll made it all the more meaningful. That did not keep him from marching right over to Noll, though, when Joe Greene felled offensive lineman Paul Howard with a cheap shot in the first half, an ignominious end to a tough 1977 for the Steelers.

I HAD A SPECIAL week that week, because we knew we were in for a battle. When you watched Pittsburgh on film, if it were a regular film, you might find yourself dozing off. A lot of what they did was repetitive. But for coaches, I guarantee you, we find that kind of thing exciting. How they get all their players to play with good fundamentals every time. How they show so much discipline. As a coach, you understand how hard it is to get 11 guys to play like that on every play. They didn't have a great year but you could still see that they had their way of playing. So I told our guys from the start that this was going to be different. In a game like that, you never know what is going to make the difference, and it is probably going to be mistakes. I told them, we have got to play every play like it is the climax play. You had to keep your head in there the whole time. No mistakes. We scored 34 points that game, we were pretty good, too. We were on a roll. We had some confidence.

The play that everybody remembers is Joe Greene going after Howard. We just saw Howard on the ground, then we figured out what had happened. That was an abnormal situation. I went to the sideline at halftime, I let them know that you don't do that in a game. I didn't say it that nicely. In fact, I said it maybe a lot harsher with my language, if you know what I mean. I respected Pittsburgh, but it was not something I was going to stand for and I told them that. They said in the paper it was a blow to his stomach but I thought it was right to his you-know-where. That was bad and I let them know it. I walked all the way across the field and let George Perles and Chuck and the coaches know that is not going to happen again or we were going to have a 22-man fight. But I knew Joe and I liked Joe. He was a heck of a player, and I couldn't understand why he did that. He was a tough, tough player, but not dirty like that. They were not used to getting beat in the playoffs, and that was probably part of it, the frustration level they felt.

Joe Collier was the defensive coordinator, and I give him a lot of credit. He and I had been together at Western Illinois, we had been on the same staff with the New England Patriots and on and on. He helped me get that job. So we had a lot of trust in each other. He is a hell of a coach, and he had that defense ready to play. We had four linebackers that, you could not find four who were of that caliber on one team, back then or even now. Tom Jackson, what a game he had. I was so happy for him. He was very, very up for that game and it showed. But it was Pittsburgh. It was a lot of hard work.

SECTION 3

BACK ON TOP

CHAPTER 8

SUPER BOWL XIII:
DALLAS, PART II

	1	2	3	4	OT	Final
Steelers	7	14	0	14		35
Cowboys	7	7	3	14		31

By Week 6 of the newly expanded, 16-week 1978 NFL season, the Steelers had already shown that they'd packed up the controversy, distraction, and bad fortune that derailed both 1976 and 77. In the throes of a 31-7 drubbing laid on Atlanta at Three Rivers Stadium, Terry Bradshaw was spied sending big smiles and waves to his wife at the time, figure skater JoJo Starbuck, who was sitting in the stands. Chuck Noll jokingly called Bradshaw over to the sideline and told him to knock it off with the googly-eyes. "(Noll) was smiling when he said it," Lynn Swann told reporters. "After all, he has often said, 'Let's make Sunday fun-day.'"

There was no shortage of fun. The Steelers got off to a franchise-best 7-0 start, rolling through some lightweight teams along the way. The early returns seemed to confirm Noll's approach to the offseason, which was simply to chalk up a couple of disappointing years to self-inflicted distractions, problems that could be easily avoided in the coming season. Noll made no major offseason moves, counting on a return to the level of concentration and seriousness of purpose that had been a hallmark of the Steelers in their first two Super Bowl seasons. It helped, too, that Pittsburgh's Steel Curtain returned to form. The Steelers led the league in points allowed (12.2 per game) and were third in yardage allowed.

At the same time, the Steelers changed their offense thanks to a rule change that, oddly enough, was inspired by a Steeler defensive player, cornerback Mel Blount, whose physical style of play was known as bump-and-run defense—which involved far more bumping than running. There were no rules in place preventing defensive players from making contact with receivers anywhere on the field. In order to spare receivers and help the passing game, the NFL installed what became known as the "Mel Blount rule," in 1977, preventing contact with receivers beyond the first five yards of the line of scrimmage, but it was not until 1978 that the effects of the rule really set in for offenses around the league.

Mike Siani

Siani was among those who frequently felt the effects of Blount's physicality and shows why the Mel Blount rule was aptly titled.

MY VERY FIRST game as a professional, we played the Steelers in Pittsburgh, the first game of the season in 1972. I wasn't even starting, Cliff Branch was starting on one side and Freddy Biletnikoff was starting on the other side. I substituted, I went in and out. We were losing, I think it was 27-0 (it was 27-7) and I was able to catch two touchdowns and finish the game with four catches and 100-and-something yards (111). I did not even know who I was playing against or how good the guy was I was playing against. It happened to be Mel Blount, who turns out to be a Hall of Famer.

If you remember back then, there were no bump rules, you could get hit anywhere on the field back then. The defensive backs, the linebackers, they could hit you anywhere and everywhere, and they did, no matter where you were. The first time I saw Mel, he was so big, I thought he was a linebacker. He was like 6-4, 215. I thought, the only way I am going to get by this guy is to beat him at the line of scrimmage because he was one yard off the ball right in my face. I was able to get by him a couple times, and he had never seen me, he had never played against me, I never played against him. So I was able to use a couple of moves and get by him and get down the sidelines. I think I surprised him.

As you released off the line of scrimmage, it was not a gentle little nudge he gave you. It was like a right cross to the chin or left cross depending on which side you tried to get by him on. It was more like a clothesline, he would hit you right between your chin and your shoulder pads, which was legal then, you could hit guys wherever you wanted. There were a couple of times I didn't get by him, there were times I wound up lying on the ground. That was the way they played defense. They figured if you were on the ground, you could not catch a pass, you were not going to get one thrown to you. That was the way the bump-and-run was played back then, and that was why corners were so big back then.

He wasn't a talker. He wouldn't knock you down and then abuse you or taunt you or make fun or anything like that. He was more businesslike than anything. And mean. They had Mean Joe Greene, but they also had Mean Mel Blount out there. He didn't like it when you caught a pass against him.

I remember in the Ice Bowl there in 1975, I actually started that game because Freddy Biletnikoff got hurt. I started on one side, and Cliff Branch started on the other, but we would switch sides, right side and left side. The very first time I lined up against Mel in that game, I mean it was just a brawl. Punches flying, I knew what he was going to do so instead of just letting him get his hands on me and jamming me and knocking me down, I said I am going to defend myself and hit him first. We got into a little brouhaha out there, as they say.

With the new rule, the Steelers expanded their passing game, putting more faith in a now-healthy Bradshaw to not only hurl the occasional long ball, but to work short-yardage underneath routes that Swann and John Stallworth could turn into big gainers. Bradshaw responded by throwing for 182.2 yards per game, a career high, and leading the league with 28 touchdown passes (20 of which went to either Swann or Stallworth). And the league rewarded him: Bradshaw was named MVP. The Steelers finished the season 14-2, and plowed through the AFC playoffs with little resistance from Denver (33-10) or Houston (34-5). Their Super Bowl foe: the Cowboys, again, but this time with a more varied offensive attack and a lot more defensive experience. If the best rivalries are those forged when the most is at stake, a second Super Bowl showdown with Dallas would ensure decades of virulence between Steeler backers and those pulling for America's Team.

Roger Staubach

Of the eight Super Bowls played in the 1970s before the 1978 season, four had been won by either the Cowboys or the Steelers, and the 1978 game was slated to settle the score between the two. There was considerable jabber between the two teams heading into the game, including Thomas Henderson picking at an old wound for Bradshaw, when he said that Bradshaw couldn't spell C-A-T if you spotted him the C and the A. Bradshaw and the Steelers, like Staubach's Cowboys, opened the game with mostly sloppy play in the first half, but the teams were knotted at 14 each in the second quarter when Staubach drove his offense to the Pittsburgh 32-yard line with just 1:52 to play before the half. But that was when Steelers defensive back Mel Blount recognized a play call that had gone for Cowboys touchdowns earlier in that game, as well as three years earlier in Super Bowl X. Blount made, as Staubach remembers it, an especially shrewd read.

BEFORE THAT GAME, that was when Henderson gave Bradshaw a hard time—he said Terry couldn't spell *cat* and that sort of thing. That probably wasn't too smart. Bradshaw was a great quarterback and he had had a great year. People don't realize about Bradshaw—they realize he won a lot of games, but they don't realize how good he really was. He just made plays whenever he had to make plays, all four years they won the Super Bowl. That's not an accident, that's just how good he was. He did that in both of the games he played against us. He made big plays, and they had a leader on the offense, in Bradshaw, and a leader on the defense, in Lambert, and that made such a big difference for them. They had great players on both sides of the ball, but it was those leaders who made those great players play at a level that they were able to achieve.

We moved the ball decently. At the beginning, Tony (Dorsett) was running pretty well. But they were usually really good at stopping the run. I felt that if I could just get enough time to get the ball out to Tony Hill and Drew and Preston Pearson and Billy Joe, we had a really good passing game that year. We led the league in almost every category in the passing game that year, and we were really a thorn in their side when it came to passing the ball.

I think a big moment, if you go back to the play before the half, I threw an interception to Blount. Coach Landry called a play-action pass, and there wasn't much time left so you knew they were not going to go for the run action. They were playing it as a pass all the way. Blount ran to the middle of the field, he anticipated that play. We had run that play twice on them for touchdowns, once in that game earlier to Drew Pearson, and once in the first Super Bowl we played against them. I talked to Mel since then, and said he knew what we were going to do, he read the play and stepped right into the play. I read the right play, and our tight end went underneath, so when I got off the field, Landry said that Blount had intercepted so Billy Joe Dupree must have been wide open. I said, 'Hey, Coach, you know, I just knew that somebody was out there.'

The defense was what they called a double-kick where the safeties go back and the cornerbacks come up. So Blount went to the middle of the field and Dirt Winston went out on Billy Joe Dupree. When I saw someone out there, I just saw someone and I thought it was Blount on him, and that meant Drew had Jack Lambert covering him, which was a mismatch. So I made the throw to Drew, and next thing I knew, Blount was making the catch. Billy Joe hit him and they called a 15-yard penalty on that. That gave them a chance to score before the half. Rocky Bleier made a heck of a catch just before the half, but remember, it was Bradshaw who made the throw. He did what he always does, and that's make the big play. They go into the locker room up 21-14 instead of 14-14, or with us having the lead. We could have gone in a touchdown or at least a field goal ahead, but I threw an interception.

Charlie Waters

The first time that the Cowboys had seen the Steelers in the Super Bowl, Pittsburgh had essentially won the game on long passes to Lynn Swann, whose leaping catches from that game remain iconic NFL moments. But by 1978, the opening of the Steelers offense to quick passes to Swann and Stallworth was obvious. Early in the second quarter, Stallworth broke open a 10-yard pass from Bradshaw and dodged groping Cowboys— particularly defensive backs Aaron Kyle and Randy Hughes—as he turned it into a 75-yard touchdown that tied the game, 7-7.

WHEN WE PLAYED them in 1978, we did watch the films that were more current, we watched their recent films and we were able to study them a little closer. But what was interesting in the film is that you really saw it. The flex defense really is designed to be a thinking defense, you have the tackles lining up behind the line, a couple yards behind the line and they protect the middle linebacker, and that extra room gives them space to diagnose the play and make a decision. The funny thing was, Tom Landry designed it to stop the great Packers running game, with outside sweeps where they would have two guards pull. It worked for that. But as teams started throwing the ball a little more, the flex defense became a little more obsolete. I am sure the Steelers picked up on that.

They were more of a short-yardage passing team in that game. They got yards after the catch. They changed a little bit with the game. They threw nice, precise, high-percentage routes, which was the way the league was going. In that game, Stallworth had a short-yard catch that he turned into a 75-yard touchdown. Aaron Kyle was right there, he could have made that tackle, I had him, too, or so I thought. I missed on him, somebody knocked him off the tackle. That was uncharacteristic of us, we were not the kind of team that let short passes turn into long touchdowns. We did not mind people getting short catches on us, but we usually got them down. Stallworth was difficult though, because he had long, strong legs, his leg lift was huge. He was a very strong man, and once he got going, he was very hard to bring down.

Cliff Harris

Harris was at the line of scrimmage when he saw Stallworth make the catch near the right hash marks and hustled to bring Stallworth down before he could score on the play, coming up just a few yards short.

STALLWORTH IS RUNNING across the middle, horizontally, on the field, and then he takes off vertically, going down and in at a 90-degree angle. He catches the ball in the middle of the field and starts to head vertical, as they say. I am coming from the line of scrimmage and I am trying my best to catch—running as fast as I can—to catch Stallworth. He had a head start on me, he is 10 or 15 yards down the field. He jukes, and I am closing the gap, closing the gap and I chase Stallworth 30 or 40 yards into the end zone for a touchdown. The announcers say, 'Well, Cliff Harris got beat on that.' Well no, I did not get beat on that! But it looked like, because I was chasing him, that he was my guy. It could have been any of the other defensive backs, because I was man-to-man on one of the guys right at the line of scrimmage, so I changed and chased him all the way to the end zone.

Larry Cole

Probably the most memorable play of Super Bowl XIII was one that was not made—the dropped pass in the end zone by Cowboys tight end Jackie Smith, who was wide open on a third-and-3 play from the Steelers' 10-yard line. The play came at the end of the third quarter and would have tied the game at 21. Instead, Dallas kicked a field goal, and the score was 21-17.

WE ALL FELT for Jackie. He was a great, great guy, and he helped us out in that season, even though he was sort of at the tail end of his career. I got to know him a little bit. We would go out to dinner a lot, me and Charlie and D.D. Lewis and Jackie, and he just really enjoyed being in Dallas, we had competed against him so long because he had so many great years in St. Louis. When this happened, he felt so bad about it, he hardly ever showed his face around Dallas fans, and that didn't need to be. I don't think the fans were very fair to him. We had a lot worse mistakes than that in that game, in other games. It was not all on him. But when you lose, the plays that you miss over a game, that is what you remember.

Roger Staubach

For Staubach, it was what happened just after Smith's would-be touchdown that stung the most. After a pair of punts, Terry Bradshaw drove the Steelers to their own 44-yard line and dropped back to pass on a second-down play. His pass floated, and as Lynn Swann—his intended receiver—and Cowboys defensive back Benny Barnes angled for the ball, Swann appeared to get his legs tangled and hit the turf. While one referee had a clear look at the play and ruled it an incomplete pass, Fred Swearingen (of Immaculate Reception fame) stepped in and called pass interference on Barnes, a controversial play that gave Pittsburgh the ball on Dallas's 23-yard line.

IT WAS 21-14 at the end of the third quarter, and we would have tied the game on Jackie's touchdown, but we still got the field goal and that made it 21-17. So, four points going into the fourth quarter, I think we still liked our chances, we really had the momentum in the third quarter. But the play that made it very difficult was, we held them again and then they get the interference call on Lynn Swann. That really hurt because they went in and scored.

The Steelers were a great team so I am not going to say that play made all the difference. But the referee who was right there called it incomplete, he was watching the play. It was the guy in the middle, Fred Swearingen, who came in from the middle of the field and threw the flag. That actually had something to do with changing the flag deal, the rules that now say you can throw a flag and talk with the other refs and pick up the flag. Back then, if you threw the flag you had to honor the flag, even if everyone else thought you were wrong. It could have gone either way, but the guy who was right there—if you look at the film you can see it—he is showing incomplete pass. Again, there were a lot of plays in that game that could have changed for both of us. That set up a score for them.

And on the next kick, (Roy) Gerela slipped on the kickoff and he wound up sort of squibbing the ball. It went right to Randy White, who was not only a defensive lineman, but also had a broken hand with a cast on it. He fumbled it, and they score again. So the game turned back in their favor when they scored those two touchdowns. The Swann play, and getting the ball back on the next kickoff. We came back—we had Tony Hill and Drew and Preston Pearson, we had one of the best teams we had in the 11 years I played. I think we made it a game, but things changed so much when they got those two touchdowns and we just didn't have enough time to come back and make it up. So it was a good game, but the score didn't indicate how it went from 21-17 right out to 35-17.

Charlie Waters

The touchdown that followed the interference call on Benny Barnes has long bothered Charlie Waters. That's because he and Cliff Harris had worked out a bit of trickery to induce a turnover from the Steelers—if only they could get Bradshaw to make the reads they were expecting him to make, the ones good football sense would seem to dictate he should make. But not only did Bradshaw not make those reads, he called a running play to Franco Harris that wound up putting a referee square in Waters's path to stop Harris from scoring. The play raises the age-old question around Bradshaw: did Bradshaw really succeed because of raw ability and blind luck, or was he a lot slier than he let on?

WE HAD A fascinating play, the play that has bothered me all my life, I still think about it. Cliff and I ran the defense. It was third and 9, third and long, and we are talking about how we're approaching it— are you going to take the tight end and I will help on the receiver, are we going to double on the tight end, are we playing man-to-man? It was easy enough to figure out because the Steelers always ran 11-personnel—that is two backs, two receivers, a tight end. Basic. So it is third and long, it is at the 20, 22-yard line. They had run, on every third down before that, they had run pressure turnouts based on our man-to-man coverage, so if we were single-covering on a wide receiver out there, the corner would take the inside away, Cliff and I would take the tight end, and the wide receiver would run a pressure turnout to the outside. If one of us went to the tight end, the tight end would do the pressure turnout as well. It was common for receivers to do that, they're just reacting to the defense.

Cliff and I had won a game by playing around with our defense on that kind of play against the Cardinals, against Jim Hart. It was a defensive play we just kind of made up as we went—we did not waste our time trying to explain it to the other guys on the field or to Coach Landry, we just figured that between the two of us, Cliff and I could work out what we want to do. What we did was, we wanted Terry to throw a pressure turnout to the tight end. So we had to show him a defense that would make him think to make that read at the line. Cliff ran over to the wide receiver when the Steelers got to the line, and made it seem like he was helping on the receiver. I was lined up on the inside of the tight end, which meant he would be open to the outside and he would run the pressure turnout. Our plan was for Cliff to move back to the ball as the throw was coming and intercept it before it got to the tight end.

Terry gets to the line of scrimmage and we start giving him all the signs. Cliff hauling ass toward the wide receiver, I am on the inside of the tight end, Randy Grossman, by myself. We wanted Terry to see this. It is an important visual for him to see Cliff out there running that hard, it is a good sales job. Once Terry saw where Cliff was and where I was, he was supposed to read what we were doing. Like I said, it worked against the Cardinals, because Jim Hart was a smart guy and read our defense and called the right thing. Cliff and I just outthought him there. Terry gets to the line of scrimmage, sees Cliff cheating to the receiver, sees me inside of Grossman and at that point, he is just supposed to call that tight end pressure turnout. Instead, third and long, he calls a damn draw play. He called for Franco Harris to run the ball on third and long.

Now I have got to make the tackle. What Cliff and I used to do, because we had a lot of responsibility in our run-defense, we would usually run eight-man fronts on running plays, so we were coming up a lot and we needed to get through the middle sometimes. So we would, before the play, go by and tap the back judge, because he is used to lining up behind the linebackers. We would go by and tap him, just warn him so he knew where we were and let him know if he was in our way, we were going to knock the shit out of him. We would do it a lot early on, so the ref was used to it, and he does not want to get hit of course. Well, we didn't do that in that game. It was the Super Bowl, everything was different and we just forgot, we just didn't do it. Good time for that.

Make matters worse, I see what Terry has called and I know it could be a disaster if Franco Harris scored a touchdown, but he did. I was in position to make a play, maybe stop him short of the first down, make them kick a field goal and, OK, we still have some life. But then I am running for Franco and the referee backs into me. I thought I was tackling Franco. Instead, I got blocked by the ref. There is a picture of me on my knees, I was bracing myself because I thought I was tackling Franco Harris, and I thought I could do that before the first down. But the official backs into me, and I knock him down and my eyes are on Franco all the way and he runs right by me, all I could do was watch. The referee was on the ground and no one touches Franco. I looked at Cliff and he looked at me like, 'What in hell?'

I asked Terry after the game, we were friends. I saw him in the hotel the next day. I said to him, 'What were you doing? Why were you running a trap to Franco? Didn't you see Cliff trying to bait you into throwing the pressure turnout to the tight end?' He turned to me and said, 'Charlie, do you think we really care what you and Cliff are doing? I don't read you guys. If Stallworth is open, I throw to Stallworth. If Swannie is open, I throw to Swannie. I don't care what you two are doing back there.' That just shattered me, I still laugh about it, I know he was joking but only a little. Because there is so much strategy in football, and Cliff and I were working so hard to figure everything out. I was saying, 'This is the NFL, you can't say that to me!' There is all this strategy, there is all this thinking going on, and he comes up to me and says he was not even paying attention. And he audibled to a trap! On third and nine. But that was Terry. He loved for you to think he is a dumb-ass, he was fine with that. But he was a lot smarter than that. He was smart and knew how to play. And Cliff and I were sure we could fool him. The best laid plans of mice and men, though.

Roger Staubach

The touchdown by Franco Harris and, immediately after the fumbled kickoff by Randy White, another by Lynn Swann put the Steelers up, 35-17. The Cowboys, as they'd done in Super Bowl X, mounted a quick-strike late-game comeback, cutting the lead to 35-31 after two touchdown passes from Staubach in the final three minutes. But when Dallas's last onside kick was recovered by Rocky Bleier, all that was left for the Steelers was to take a knee and lay claim to their third Super Bowl trophy.

I REMEMBER BRADSHAW COMING over and giving me a hug after the game, and I was thinking, 'My God, I don't want a hug.' I mean, I am not a sore loser, I think, but I don't like to lose. That became a picture they show a lot in the highlights, and I still don't like seeing that. But we respected them. They respected us. We threw some words back and forth in those days, maybe more before the 1975 Super Bowl, but I think our respect grew over time. I didn't like the mouthing off that took place, but it just happened.

Our 1978 team was one of our best teams, and we were healthy. We were really good. Unfortunately, they were just a little bit better than us. I would not say they were much better than us, but they won. I used to kid Joe Montana, I have seen him a few times, and he won four Super Bowls. I won two, I was 2-2, but I would say to him, 'Hey, Joe, why don't you try to beat the Steelers next time instead of the Bengals twice and Buffalo?' He laughed, but it's the truth. I hate losing two Super Bowls, but I really feel like I lost to one of the greatest teams of all time. But it was just that we let them have too many chances, getting 35 points. Offensively, we were playing against one of the best defenses of all time. They were just a really great team. I think that those Steelers teams that played in that era, winning those four Super Bowls that they won, they were the greatest team that ever played in the NFL. Look at both sides of the ball, with Franco, Bradshaw, the receivers they had, Swann and Stallworth, the offensive line. And then the defense. I mean, the games we lost, they were tough losses for us. But for them, both sides of the ball, they just really brought it all together, both sides of the ball, great coaching as well.

I would rank them up there with the best in NFL history, and we just happened to run into them at that time. We were a great team too, but that second loss to the Steelers sort of cost us the Team of the 70s title, they won the four Super Bowls in that decade. Still, we played pretty well against one of the best teams of all time.

CHAPTER 9

SUPER BOWL XIV: ONE MORE TIME

	1	2	3	4	OT	Final
Steelers	3	7	7	14		31
Rams	7	6	6	0		19

On October 28, 1979, almost exactly nine months after the Steelers held off the Cowboys in Super Bowl XIII, Dallas and Pittsburgh met again, this time in Week 9 at Three Rivers Stadium. By this point, with the two teams having squared off for two championships, the publicly accepted tropes assigned to the identities of each of the teams were assigned and accepted. The Steelers were the roughneck brutes, all heft and scars, the types who would show up at a garden party in flannel and bearing a warm 12-pack of Iron City beer. The Cowboys were the thinkers, adherents to the scientific method, endlessly running computer models that could somehow find the algorithm that would reveal the right strategy, the right formation, the right play. The stereotype wasn't quite right—the Steelers were smarter than they got credit for, and the Cowboys could be physical with the best of them—but it provided an entertaining dimension to their matchups.

Still, when they went to Pittsburgh in mid-1979, the Cowboys did little to diminish their reputation for imposing excessive thought in what is, basically, a game of choreographed rampage. Dallas resorted to nearly every form of football trickery available. They ran a fake punt from their own 31 (it failed), they tried a halfback option pass (that failed, too), and they even set up a Statue of Liberty play with Tony Dorsett that was called back because of a penalty. "That computer down there in Dallas must be smokin'," end Dwight White said. "I'd say that if any group needed to be convinced about the Pittsburgh Steelers, it was the Dallas Cowboys. And being the intelligent people I know them to be, I know the Cowboys will admit it."

Countering the Cowboys' razzle-dazzle was the Chuck Noll special, the play the Steelers had been using for the entire decade Emperor Chaz had been in Pittsburgh: the 35 Trap. That was the call on two of Pittsburgh's most important offensive plays, an eight-yard touchdown by Rocky Bleier and a 48-yard rush by Franco Harris. The Steelers slammed the Cowboys, 14-3, a score that hardly reflects their dominance. Linebacker Dirt Winston summed it up, quoted in *Sports Illustrated*: "It's better to hit than to think. The man who thinks out there is lost." Pittsburgh rolled through the season free of controversy and building on the offensive advances they'd made the previous season. The Steelers led the NFL in points and yardage in 1979—offensive points and yardage, that is, not their usual defensive domination in those categories. The defense held steady, ranking second in yardage allowed and fifth in points. The Steelers wrapped up 12-4, blew out Miami in their divisional-round playoff game (34-14), and fought off the Oilers in the conference championship (27-13). Dallas was again expected to be the Super Bowl foe, but the heavily favored Cowboys were stunned at home by the Rams, a team that was just 9-7 in the regular season and carried a reputation for flopping in the big moments. L.A. shut out Tampa Bay in the conference championship, 9-0, and earned its first trip to the Super Bowl.

Fred Dryer

Defensive Lineman

Teams: New York Giants, 1969-71; Los Angeles Rams, 1972-81

Dryer had joined the Rams from the Giants in 1972, a Pro Bowl book-end for Rams star end Jack Youngblood, and helped anchor a defense that had finished in the Top 4 in yardage and points allowed for six straight seasons from 1973 to 1978 but had begun to drop off in 1979—which made their appearance in the Super Bowl all the more baffling. The Rams certainly knew they were sizable underdogs in the game and were portrayed as a team that was feeling disrespected heading into the game.

FROM OUR STANDPOINT, we got to the Super Bowl with not one of our better teams. But like most people in that tournament, whoever gets hot at the right time is going to be the one who has the most success. We always thought that we could match up with any team in the league and Pittsburgh was no exception. We thought we matched up well with them. We were convinced that we not only could but would beat them. We shut out Tampa Bay in the playoffs, and after that game, the line came out, the betting line, and it showed that we were 13-point underdogs. There was no way I could see that. But we were not that bothered by it, we were not sitting around feeling disrespected. I don't know if that was press generated or if that was real. Everybody has to be confident in their own way. It comes out in those situations like sound-bites. Anything that they said, anything that was in the newspapers and magazines, we did not take that as a sign like, 'Well they said this and this, so now we have got to play extra hard.' We were going to play hard no matter what, and live with the results.

Even if it was not our best team, we had a good and experienced defensive front. Our approach was that the Steelers always seemed to understand that the sport is defined at the line of scrimmage. Our goal in that game was to take the line of scrimmage away from them. If we were going to beat them, we would have to beat them at the things they did best. And we did. We figured, if we could just allow them minimal yardage per series, that would be all right. We kind of wanted them to throw the ball, we just did not want them to run those quick running plays they got all the time. We wanted to control the line. They were very efficient at the point of attack and at the line of scrimmage, but we did a very good job of playing our fundamentals, playing our techniques and winning those battles at the point of attack. That was critical to us. After that, it would just come down to the breaks, it would come down to hoping our offense could hold onto the ball and move it.

Jackie Slater

Slater was only twenty-five and in his fourth season when he arrived at Super Bowl XIV with a difficult assignment: handle left end L.C. Greenwood. Around the NFL, Greenwood had established himself as a first-rate pass rusher, but what was worse for an offensive lineman like Slater was that Greenwood had established himself as a showman. Entering the game, as much as he was worried about Greenwood's technique, Slater was worried about the image of Greenwood celebrating over a sacked Rams quarterback.

L.C. GREENWOOD AT that time was probably one of the most charismatic personalities to play in a Super Bowl, especially on the defensive line. I mean, this guy was dancing over everybody's quarterback, you know, and who wants that? This is way before Mark Gastineau. He did that and didn't draw the scorn of society or the rest of the guys around the National Football League. If it is possible, he did it in a classy way. People didn't mind. He was a competitor, he did it hard and he was just trying to beat you. L.C. Greenwood, he was special—6-6, about 265 or whatever it was, rangy, long arms. One of those guys you just couldn't pin down. Quickness and speed with range, he was a different kind of a guy to deal with. Certain body builds are predisposed to be able to do certain things and not be able to other things. To me, the perception was that if you were a long-limbed guy, the probability of you being a real quick, change-of-direction guy and power guy, were not very likely. But L.C. was deceptive that way to me, because he could take one step, and he would be on you, in a different spot with his quickness. If you just jumped around casually to get in front of him, he could beat you with his power.

All I could see was this guy dancing over my quarterback. That is what I was focused on—what can I do to keep this guy from making plays? I went into the game, I can't say I had a game plan but I knew what I wanted to try to do. But it was a game as young guy, not having a lot of experience, it was a game where I figured I would have to figure a lot of things out on the fly. I was awed by his experience, almost overwhelmed by his persona, who he was, the way he carried himself in that Steel Curtain defense. He was respected by those guys, he was a leader. In fact, I got to meet him before he passed away at the Hall of Fame induction, and even then, his personality was just the way I had imagined. He was very quietly, and sometimes overtly, confident. He had a confidence in himself that was all innate, it was who he was.

But during the Super Bowl, he didn't say a word. He was supremely focused. It was a little unsettling to me to see how much he wanted to beat you. This guy came to win the game. I had gotten into a bit of a groove against him, I was keeping him off the quarterback, I was keeping him at bay on rundowns. But at a crucial time in the game, I thought I could get him while he was playing an outside front. So I head-faked him, twice, just to get him to jump out there, and what he did, he went down inside and hit the back about a yard-and-a-half in the backfield and just made an outstanding play. The thing I remember about that was, here I am a first-year starter, I am in my first big game and I am trying to trick a seasoned veteran like L.C. Greenwood with a head fake? When I look back on it, I am like, you must have been out of your mind, he didn't fall for any of that.

Jack Youngblood

Defensive Lineman

Team: Los Angeles Rams, 1971-84

Jack Youngblood earned six Pro Bowl honors in his Hall of Fame career, but of all his accomplishments, his very appearance in Super Bowl XIV and the championship game before it might be the most impressive. That's because Youngblood had broken his fibula during the Rams' upset over the Cowboys, and rather than letting it heal as any good patient would, Youngblood told doctors to tape the leg up so he could go back and play. He did. Three weeks later, he suited up for the Super Bowl—and also took some teammates on a hunting trip back home in Florida, in addition to playing in the Pro Bowl.

YOU HAVE GOT to remember, we had some wonderful guys and we had been together a long time and that was one of the keys to our success that year. But the thing about us was, not to be demeaning, but we could not get one quarterback who could consistently get the job done. We either got them hurt or we swapped them out or they just couldn't get it done. We had a running game, we had an offensive line, we had fast wide receivers who could make plays, we had a defense that over the course of the 70s, we outperformed the Pittsburgh defense. You look at our records and for that decade, we were 12-2, 10-4, in that range for six straight years. The '79 team was 9-7. We went through three quarterbacks.

(The leg injury) was the worst thing that could have happened to me at the time. It was the worst possible injury, for me, at that time. To have the opportunity to be in the Super Bowl, playing the Steelers, after we had been trying to get through that door, that final door for the last eight years or so, for me that was really bad timing. For me not to be able to make a difference the way I thought should be able to, that was hard. I got the job done, I did my job, but I was supposed to make a difference in a game like that, and I was not able to make a difference. You hate to say you regret something, but I regret that that happened.

The only concern that the doctors had was that I stayed on it for three weeks, and I did not let the body heal itself. So that calcium could solidify as it was and it would basically heal incorrectly and it would be a situation where you were hurting that particular spot over and over. In today's world, they would have pinned it down with a plate right after the Dallas game, but I was able to get them to let me keep playing. But just to give you an idea of that era, and how crazy I was when I played, after the Super Bowl, the Pro Bowl was the next weekend, so what did I do? I went to the Pro Bowl and played. And everybody asks me, why did you go to the Pro Bowl with a broken leg? I said, hell, I was not going to miss the party. I went through 17 ballgames, I lost in the Super Bowl, our team lost, the Pro Bowl is your party afterward. I was not going to miss that.

Funny thing is, I would always take the boys, five or six of us, we would go back to Monticello, my hometown in Florida, and I would take the boys hunting and fishing after the season. We went quail hunting one day—before I got my leg fixed up—and we were walking through what we call wire grass, it's about knee-deep. I did not see this gopher hole. I stepped in the gopher hole, not with my good leg, but with my bad leg, and I went down like someone shot me. I am lying in the grass, the boys are out in the field and I go down and I start hollering and screaming. They all look around and they could not see me. And they're all going, 'Where are you, what is going on?' And I was thinking, I go from the Super Bowl, playing the Pittsburgh Steelers, to lying in a bunch of wire grass, hollering, in just a couple days? I thought maybe I should start to take it easy.

Fred Dryer

Not having Youngblood at 100 percent on the left side of the defensive line made things more difficult for Dryer on the right side, particularly in pass protection.

JACK'S INJURY WAS tough. He broke a small bone in his lower leg, but he played through it, he was not going to miss that Super Bowl, he played valiantly. But Pittsburgh knew what was going on and the way they changed their game plan for it was, a portion of the time, they singled on Jack in pass protection, and slid everything out toward me. So I have Jon Kolb on my side and he is a big tackle, but they are also sliding the guard over to push out against me, he would pick me up, too, and slide the pass protection over. If Jack is healthy, they've got to double-team him. The blocking combinations are different and that would allow the rest of us to be more aggressive. They had a tight end on Jack's side most of the time, and he would release. So they almost forced Jack to line head-up on the tackle and it was tough for him to play at full speed, because it was a painful thing for him. What we wound up doing was running a lot of blitzes, pushing people up the middle especially as they came across the field. But that would not normally have been our game plan.

If the Rams' goal had been to control the line of scrimmage, the first half went according to plan. They controlled the line of scrimmage, giving Franco Harris very little running room and holding

Pittsburgh to just 10 points and a 13-10 Rams lead. In film sessions, the Rams had been paying attention to Terry Bradshaw's audible tendencies, and after the game, center Mike Webster said, "When we'd audible, (linebacker) Jack Reynolds would call the correct defense for the play we audibled to. They knew us."

Fred Dryer

But the Rams knew more than just the Steelers' audibles—they'd picked up the tendencies of Franco Harris, which very often gave away the play Pittsburgh was about to run. That was a big factor in limiting Harris to only 46 yards on 20 carries. In all, the Steelers tried 37 running plays and gained only 84 yards, an average of 2.3 yards per play.

EVERYTHING WAS GOING the way we hoped and the way we thought it might up until the middle of the fourth quarter. We worked very, very hard to control the line of scrimmage, our fundamentals and our techniques. It was where things started for us. Our big people could cover their big people, that was always our goal. You can run defenses where you are bringing guys up and shooting gaps that way, but you can't do that as a steady diet, it will kill you. We always wanted to cover the center, and that was, for them, Mike Webster. So we tried to do that, it takes him out of the play, makes him do what you want him doing, not what they want him doing. Most of the time, when you put a man on the center, someone is coming over to help him, one of the guards. Once that guy blocks down on the nose tackle, the linebacker steps up and we have guys who can make plays.

What we were doing was to put the front up there to get the offense to run the play we wanted them to run. We want to cover the center, we want you to use the off guard to help block the nose tackle. What Pittsburgh tried to do, they ran the 31X play to Franco Harris between the guard and center. We watched all of their films and we found something where, he would cheat and try to get one half-step behind the quarterback so he had a straight shot coming into the '01' hole. Instead of being a little bit to the right, behind the guard in that formation, he cheated. Every time you saw him cheating, you knew they were going to run that '01' play, and every time they ran that play, we put a guy right on the center and took the center right out of the game. It's like having a tell in poker. Every team has a personality, the great thing about the sport is that it is a puzzle. Each play has its nuances and appearances, and what you are trying to do is figure out what is going on before it happens, whether it is the way a player moves or something the quarterback says or how a guy comes out of the huddle and where he is looking. Franco had that tell and we had a lot of success in stopping him when we faced him in part because it was an important play for them.

With so much trouble running the ball in the first half, the Steelers turned to another old staple of their Super Bowl offenses: the deep ball to their wide receivers, much as they'd done when Lynn Swann dominated in Super Bowl X. In the first half, Bradshaw attempted only four passes to either Swann or John Stallworth, and completed three, all for short yardage—Swann had caught two balls for 22 yards, and Stallworth had just one catch for three yards. But on their first possession of the second half, Bradshaw threw deep to Swann, who leaped and split defensive backs Nolan Cromwell and Pat Thomas to make a 47-yard touchdown catch.

Jack Youngblood

In the wake of Swann's touchdown, the Rams responded with a touchdown drive of their own, covering 77 yards in less than 90 seconds and putting L.A. into the lead, 19-17, with a little more than 10 minutes to go in the third quarter.

THE PLAY TO Lynn Swann, he must have leaped 14 feet in the air. I swear, I can still see it and I don't know how he caught that. And poor Pat Thomas, because Pat and Nolan had double-coverage on him, and he just outjumped both of them. They did everything right but it was a case of, that's how good Swann was. But we came right back. Our next possession, Billy Waddy had been going at their corner (Ron Johnson) all game, and he catches a 50-yard bomb, and it might have been more but he had to come back for it. Our offense lifted us right up and came up with the play, Lawrence McCutcheon throwing the halfback pass right back in the same area. We knew we could play with the big boys. We played with them for five or six years, getting to the championship game before we got the door slammed in our faces by Minnesota or Dallas. But when we finally broke through, we knew we could play with Pittsburgh. (Coach Ray) Malavasi, he was so good at putting us in the right position to make the plays, that was the big key. We had great players, too, and that made his job easier. So we thought we could play with anybody.

Fred Dryer

The Rams were not able to expand their lead in the third quarter, but they did manage to knock Lynn Swann out of the game on a leaping six-yard catch with 8:30 to play in the third. And Bradshaw seemed rife with mistakes, throwing interceptions on back-to-back possessions in Rams territory. He also threw what should have been an interception to Rams defensive back Nolan Cromwell for a touchdown in the middle of the third quarter, a play that would have put the Rams up, 26-17—if Cromwell had not dropped the pass. Had Cromwell hung onto the ball, he surely would have scored, with nothing but green grass in front of him. As Mike Webster said about the muffed interception in Sports Illustrated*: "The only thing that could have stopped him was a .357 magnum." The Rams had played well but hadn't turned their success into a comfortable lead.*

WE FELT GOOD about where we were. There was a TV timeout in that third quarter, and Terry was walking over to talk to the sideline, talk to the coaches. On the way back, Terry was going by and we were up 19-17, and it was just like they had used all their offense. We had seen everything from them. I said to him, 'So, what do you guys got left?' They had gone through their offense. They were not going to re-establish the line of scrimmage. We watched all their film that year and we knew, they had nothing left.

So Terry didn't say anything back to me, but later on he told me what they did. They went back two years in their playbook and pulled out some pass plays. They just started incorporating different plays into the game on the spot. It was funny, you could see it. If you play long enough and you're standing around, you look at the other team and you can see that look where they say, 'We better get our sh— going or we are going to lose this one.' We didn't surprise them, they knew we were a good matchup. They did not go to sleep on us. But we did see them get to the point where they were scrambling and they were down to a couple of plays that were going to make the difference.

Those games, the window of opportunity is so small. There were a couple of places there that could have changed things, there were interceptions that we dropped, that might have gone for a touchdown. There was the one by Nolan Cromwell, our safety, he was a really great defensive back, and Bradshaw turned and threw one back across the field over the middle, and I mean, there was no one in front of him between him and the end zone. That was it. Had he scored and taken it all the way, it would have been a nine-point lead in the fourth quarter. But that is what happens in games like that. You get windows of opportunity and if you don't take advantage of them, that's the difference between winning and losing.

In the fourth quarter and trailing, 19-17, the Steelers almost suddenly recognized the importance of the moment and snapped out of their funk. There were now just minutes to play, and Pittsburgh had an undefeated Super Bowl record to defend. Dryer said the Steelers dug into their old playbooks to find workable lines of attack for this Super Bowl, and they'd need to come up with something the Rams had not seen before. They again settled on a reliable plan from recent seasons, one that had worked in the previous year's Super Bowl—get the ball to John Stallworth, and let L.A. try to figure out how to defend him.

Jack Youngblood

Even with a broken bone in his leg, and even though he was not drawing the double-teams he'd typically require from the offensive line, Youngblood remained a disruptive force for the Rams throughout the game. With 12:15 to go as the Steelers lined up for a third-and-eight play from their own 27-yard line, Youngblood was prepared to pin back his ears, knowing the Steelers were in a passing situation, and get to Bradshaw. As he began his rush, Steelers tackle Jon Kolb forced him outside, but Youngblood stopped and broke inside, just as Bradshaw was getting ready to throw. When healthy, Youngblood might have made the play on Bradshaw. Instead, Bradshaw got the throw off with Youngblood bearing down on him and took advantage of a mistake in the Rams secondary, hitting Stallworth in stride over the swiping hand of Rod Perry for another deep-ball score, moving the score to 24-19.

HALF A STEP. That was all I needed and I would have hit Terry. I remember that like it was yesterday. Kolb was a tough guy even if you're completely healthy, but he was that much tougher when I was dealing with the leg. I was so close, I could almost hear him throwing the ball. Terry just heaved it down there right before I got to him. That was the one play where I thought I was going to be able to deal with the leg and still make the play. I told Bradshaw, he was on the ground after that play, and I said to him, 'You're lucky.' You know, Terry was great with the deep passes of course. But I felt like I might have gotten him, just that, every step was like someone was stabbing me in the leg. I had it taped up. We taped a piece of plastic over the area where the fibula was broken just to keep it from taking contact and getting hurt that way. But every step was like, it was reminding me it was there. I always think, if I could have just had one play where it did not bother me at all, it would have been that play. Because I think I would have gotten Terry.

FRED DRYER

Dryer was not as close to Bradshaw as Youngblood was, but he, too, might have had a clean shot at Bradshaw with just a little more time. More than that, what struck Dryer about the touchdown play was how close the Rams—or, more specifically, Perry—were to handling Bradshaw, Stallworth, and the Steelers altogether.

ITALKED TO ROD Perry about this, and he said the first touchdown to Stallworth actually touched his finger, he jumped and the ball hit his finger, but Stallworth still made the play. That was small consolation. And you always think, 'Gee whiz, if Rod had been born a half-inch taller, we might have won the [expletive] game!' But, you know, that was what the Steelers did.

JACKIE SLATER

No team in the Steelers' four-year Super Bowl run had Pittsburgh on the ropes quite like the Rams did—the Vikings had never mounted an offensive threat, the Cowboys had close scores that only tightened as Roger Staubach attempted late comebacks in Super Bowls X and XIII. But before the tide turned in the fourth quarter, before the 31-19 score began to look lopsided, the Rams really had Pittsburgh considering a loss. Slater could see that in an encounter with Bradshaw, who has since come up with the perfect rejoinder whenever Slater mentions it.

WE HAD THEM right where we wanted them. If you look at the film, we had a situation where one of our defensive backs, Terry Bradshaw had an errant throw and it hit him right in the stomach, all he had to do was catch the ball and run and he would have scored a touchdown. We had a couple of missed tackle situations that, we didn't pin them down, let them convert some. I tell Terry Bradshaw when I see him, I am one of the few people who knows what his face looks like when he is down in a big game and he thinks he is going to lose it. What happened was, I was throwing a block and I rolled over, out of bounds at the sideline. Terry was standing right there. I barked a few words at him. He had this expression on his face like, 'Man, we're losing, there's not much time.' But he came back and put a dagger in us with that 76-yard pass to Stallworth. So I tell him I know what his face looks like when he thinks he is going to lose, but he always shoots back at me real fast: 'But you lost the game.'

The Bradshaw-Stallworth touchdown was disheartening for the Rams defense, but not altogether deflating. The game had swung back and forth throughout the day, and L.A. certainly believed it could make up the 24-19 deficit when it got the ball back with 8:51 to play in regulation. But after two quick passes from Vince Ferragamo to Preston Dennard, the Rams' drive stalled, and when Ferragamo attempted to squeeze a pass to Ron Smith, Steelers linebacker Jack Lambert stepped in for the interception. Another long pass from Bradshaw to Stallworth for 45 yards on the Steelers' next drive set up a Franco Harris touchdown that pushed the score to 31-19, where it would remain.

Fred Dryer

For the Rams, 1979 was the last time Youngblood would earn a Pro Bowl spot. Dryer would play only one more year, defensive centerpiece Jack Reynolds would move on to San Francisco after the 1980 season, and Bob Brudzinski would move on to Miami. The vaunted Rams defense wouldn't be the same—though if one looked closely at the 1979 champs, it was obvious the aging Steel Curtain wouldn't be the same, either.

I WAS NEAR THE end of my career. And I remember, I was thirty-five years old, and I was looking at it like, 'If we can get this one, I will [expletive] drive home tonight and that'll be it.' They were similar. The Steelers were a great team and they had all these Hall of Famers, guys who won a lot of Super Bowls obviously, but they were getting up there in their 30s. Bradshaw and Joe Greene, some of their linemen. I played one more year after that Super Bowl and that was all for me. That's sports. A team is a bus station. People are always coming and going. And when you have a team you are hoping you catch everything at just the right time, the talent pool, the chemistry, that window of opportunity that you just hope you can take advantage of while you're all in the station, before it all changes again, before some people leave the station and new people come in. That's the reason it is so damn difficult—the influx of people, and the exit of others. That's where we were.

SECTION 4

THE RIVALRY YEARS

CHAPTER 10

"THAT WAS THE END
OF THAT RIVALRY"

FOR THE STEELERS, the win over the Rams in Super Bowl XIV could not have been more fitting. Five years earlier, Pittsburgh had beaten Minnesota in Super Bowl IX, a win for an upstart team that was probably ahead of its time, slipping through the very early opening of its championship window. But after the tight win over Los Angeles, that window was closing, and the Steelers were fortunate to come up with one last title before it slammed irreversibly shut. By the opening of the 1980 season, Terry Bradshaw was 32, and the vaunted Pittsburgh backfield of Franco Harris (30) and Rocky Bleier (34) had lost some of its zip. The entire Steelers defensive front four—L.C. Greenwood, Joe Greene, John Banaszak, and Steve Furness—was over 30, as were linebacker Jack Ham and cornerback Mel Blount (32), and safety Mike Wagner (31). The offensive line had been remade, particularly the left side, where Sam Davis retired and Jon Kolb moved to the bench.

The steady seep of age is inevitable for any great team in sports, and its effect on the Steelers was apparent in 1980, when the team finished a paltry 9-7 and wound up 12th in the league in yards allowed, the first time since 1971 that they failed to finish among the top 8 in that category. The Steel Curtain had lost some of its luster, and the established dynamics of the AFC—that is, you had to go through Pittsburgh—changed swiftly. What had been some of the Steelers' fiercest rivals, like the Dolphins, Raiders, and Cowboys, faded in importance.

A.J. Duhe

Linebacker/Defensive Lineman

Team: *Miami Dolphins, 1977-84*

A.J. Duhe was in his third season when the Dolphins went to Pittsburgh for their playoff opener in 1979, a game the Steelers controlled from start to finish thanks, mostly, to a 159-25 advantage in rushing yardage that keyed a 34-14 win. Two years later, in the second game of the season, the Steelers went to Miami for a Thursday night game and were dominated, 30-10.

WE HAD A rivalry with them to an extent, that went back to the early 1970s, but we just did not play that often after that, they were on the decline when we were coming up. I wish we would have played more, because it was a good rivalry back when the teams were so damn good. I recall when we played them in the playoffs in one of the years they went to the Super Bowl, the final year. It was a really cold day, it was nasty, it was not one of those crazy weather games you get in Pittsburgh, but it was one of those that you, if you played in Miami, the cold was a little intimidating. They jumped on us pretty good, and they were able to throw out different running backs at us and keep us on our heels. They had a lot of experience, a lot of playoff savvy, so it was a learning experience for us. We were still figuring ourselves out a little bit.

For me, the good thing was watching the film on their defensive players. I would watch guys who were good and did it right, and the Steelers had plenty of those. When I played end, you could look at a guy like Joe Greene and see his technique, how he bull-rushed, his swim move, all of those things. Then when the Dolphins switched me to linebacker, I had to learn to play that position from scratch basically. So I watched a lot of Jack Ham and Lambert, I did kind of see their style a little bit, because that was at the back end of their career so they were doing things a lot more mental than just physical, which made it better for me because I could see how they were approaching things. They were dominant players, such great players, and I would watch them when I moved to linebacker and was trying to learn the position, who better to watch than those guys? My skill set was different, they were more of your true, lean linebacker guys, 230 pounds or so. Lambert played like a mean dog, and I got that spirit from him, and Ham played the game more like, cerebral, never making mistakes, always in the right spot. Both in the Hall of Fame, so I tried to model myself after them, as sort of a combination of them.

Two years after we saw them in the playoffs, you could tell how far we had come. We kind of turned the tide a little bit, it was in one of the first Thursday night games that they started moving around Monday Night Football, it was Thursday and it was early in 1981. The weather was more like us, we were at the Orange Bowl and it was hot, it was humid, it was rainy. We won big in that game, we were probably just coming together as a team, the year before we had made the playoffs, we beat up on them pretty good. I was coming into my own, I moved to linebacker, and it was a learning curve, our defense was gelling a lot better, we were figuring out our zone-blitz scheme a lot better. We got to Terry a lot in that game, he threw some interceptions. The offensive line had changed, too. We had a lot of sacks (four total), and we also got to Terry a lot, hit him even if we did not sack him. We did a number on them, and you could see they were not happy about it, their coaches were yelling, all of that. We were the young team at the time, and I would not say they were old at that point, but they were getting older. It is a short turnaround to play on Thursday after a Sunday game, so if you're in your 30s like most of those guys were, I think that did not help them much either.

Bobby Ross

Coach

Teams: San Diego Chargers, 1992-96; Detroit Lions, 1997-2000

Ross was an assistant coach with the Chiefs in the late 1970s and early '80s, and as talented as the Steelers were, what stood out to Ross was that some of the Steelers—namely, the always ill-tempered Jack Lambert— managed to turn personal friendships into bitter rivalries when they took the field.

AS AN ASSISTANT, I was with Kansas City and we played them one year with the great, great defensive team, and I think probably the greatest defense of all time, or one of them. I remember Jack Lambert—we had a center named Jack Rudnay out of Northwestern, a really good player, he was not real big but he was a fine player. He knew Lambert from their years being in the league, playing in the Pro Bowl, things like that. I was a young coach at the time, kind of a rookie coach, my second year, and I can remember Jack Rudnay hollering out before our game, he said, 'Hey Jack, you old SOB, how're you doing?' And Lambert looked over at us, and I am going to tell you right now, there was no smile on his face. Rudnay was smiling and laughing, but Lambert had this look on him, like he was ready to, you know, bite somebody's head off. He was not smiling. I said to Rudnay, 'Jack, we got a problem today, these guys are ready to play.' Jack laughed it off like it was nothing. Well, 30 points later, it's 30-3 and that kind of shows you how that day went.

Tom Flores

After losing to the Steelers in the 1975 playoffs by a 16-10 score, the Raiders took control of the series against Pittsburgh, winning six straight against the Steelers from 1976 to 1984. Even as the dynasty faded, and with it some of the teeth-grinding, red-eyed Oakland-Pittsburgh rage of the 1970s, respect between organizations remained.

IT WAS ALWAYS fun to play them because you did not have to give too many pep talks when you played the Steelers. The players had a good sense of the rivalry, and they had respect for those teams. You had to, they were champions. Besides, in those days, there was no free agency, so you knew the guys you were playing against every year. Nobody was moving around like they do now. You would play them in the regular season and then see them after the game and say, 'OK, see you in the playoffs.' For a while there, it was the Raiders and the Steelers, every year. It almost felt like we were in the same division because we saw them so much.

Even as their guys got older, the one thing they had was continuity. I really liked the way Chuck Noll approached that. He had an idea of what he was going to do before the game and he did it, week after week. They would play against our guys, and the players would expect that they would go into the game and beat on each other, they were extremely physical players, the Steelers were known for their physicality. But so were the Raiders, and we knew we had to be at their level if we wanted to beat them. The Raiders knew they were in a street fight when they played the Steelers, especially when they went to Pittsburgh. They had that Astroturf that was more like cement, everyone would come out of there a little beaten up and bruised. Cold and icy and just really tough to play there.

Larry Cole

Cole had been part of both Cowboys-Steelers Super Bowls in the 1970s and acknowledged that the two losses were tough to accept. But lest an outside observer assume that the passion for those rivalries dies altogether upon retirement, Cole offers a reminder from 1988 that even if diminished talent and age takes away from the quality of an old rivalry on the field—that was certainly the case for the Cowboys and Steelers for most of the 1980s—it still lives on in some hearts and minds. At least, for a while.

IT'S FUNNY, MAYBE 10 years later, Andy Russell invited a bunch of us to come in to Pittsburgh and play a flag football game in Pittsburgh at the stadium, one of those charity games. For fun and for the fans. But we went into it and we just couldn't quite handle playing flag football. It was still Cowboys vs. Steelers. It wound up being a pile of injuries. Frenchy Fuqua broke his ankle. Franco Harris got hit in the face, broke his nose. Andy Russell tore his Achilles. There were maybe three of us that pulled hamstrings. Terry wasn't there but we won the game. It was stupid, of course. But that's sports, you are a competitor and you want to win. For us, it was like, we wanted to beat them somehow someway. We stayed with them that night, and hung around those guys, and they were really a great bunch of guys.

After that, though, they never had another Cowboys-Steelers flag football game again. I think that was the end of that rivalry.

Cliff Harris

Harris was part of the 1988 charity game in Pittsburgh, and it was his elbow that accidentally broke Franco Harris's nose, which inspired Cliff to send a conciliatory gift. It was another gift, from his old rival, Lynn Swann, that meant the most to Cliff in the long run.

LYNN ALWAYS SAID I was the motivating factor in his Super Bowl. So we went, after we retired, we went to Pittsburgh and played at Three Rivers Stadium against the Steelers, we had a Cowboys-Steelers flag football game. After the game, Lynn Swann came over to me and gave me his jersey and signed it, which he does not do much. He said, 'Cliff, let's swap jerseys, you were my No. 1 nemesis, and I guess I was yours. Now we're friends, let's swap jerseys.' I gave him my jersey and he gave me his. I still have it today.

In the touch football game, Bradshaw was not the quarterback, it was Terry Hanratty playing quarterback. I was playing safety, of course, and they ran Franco in a route across the middle and he curled in. And you know, we were playing flag football, and I was enjoying being there, so I went for the interception. Franco—we didn't have helmets, just shorts and our jerseys—Franco turned his head as I went up for the interception and I hit his nose with my elbow. I hit him right in the nose, because I was slower, my reaction time was not as good as it was so I mistimed it. I wasn't there in time because I wasn't as fast as I used to be. I thought I was going to miss him altogether but I actually collided with him and broke his nose. He was lying on the ground saying, 'Aw, man, Cliff, I played all these years without a broken nose and you break my nose in a dad-gum touch football game.' I said, 'I'm so sorry man, you know I did not mean to do that.' It ended up, he went to the doctor's that night and I sent him a bottle of champagne with a note after he got it fixed.

CHAPTER 11

THE AFC CENTRAL

IF THE STEELERS were no longer the AFC powerhouse they'd been for nearly a decade when the 1980s came around—and if their national-profile rivalries were not quite the same because of it—then one offshoot was the rekindling of their rivalries within the Central Division. The Steelers had division rivals in the '70s, of course, and some of those games were ferociously fought. But those rivalries were based on geography and the realities of scheduling more than on seriousness of competition. The Steelers won the Central seven out of eight times from 1972 to 1979, and in that span, Pittsburgh was 11-5 against Cincinnati; 13-4 against Houston, including a win in the 1979 playoffs; and 13-3 against Cleveland.

Once the rest of the division caught up to the Steelers, the AFC Central gained a reputation as the league's most raucous and colorful division. There would be no dynasties in this era. Between 1980 and 1993, every team in the Central won the division at least twice, including three division titles for Pittsburgh. The division was so tight in 1990 that three teams finished tied for first, and eight times over that span, the division crown was decided by one game or less. As a result, there was genuine resentment among the organizations within the division. As Oilers coach Jerry Glanville explained, "I always took great pride in the fact that, at the league meeting every year, they would take pictures of the different coaching staffs by division, so you would have AFC West and East and the NFC teams and all of that. But they never took a picture of the AFC Central at the time, they could never get us together.

I guess they figured it would wind up in a fight. That's just how it was. You won't find an AFC Central picture taken, isn't that awesome? I had a speaking engagement recently, and someone asked me how long has it been since you talked to (former Bengals coach) Sam Wyche? I said, 1987. That is how it was."

Key Rivalry Games:

October 26, 1980, at Cleveland Municipal Stadium. Browns 27, Steelers 26.

	1	2	3	4	OT	Final
Browns	0	7	7	13		27
Steelers	10	3	13	0		26

November 16, 1980, at Three Rivers Stadium. Steelers 16, Browns 13.

	1	2	3	4	OT	Final
Steelers	0	7	0	9		16
Browns	0	13	0	0		13

Don Cockroft

Kicker

Team: *Cleveland Browns, 1968-80*

Don Cockroft was a kicker for the Browns from 1968 to 1980 and the author of a book about the 1980 Browns, The 1980 Kardiac Kids. *He watched the Steelers grow into a dynasty in the '70s and was with the Browns as they helped bring down that dynasty by—shockingly— winning the Central Division in 1980, a season that featured veteran quarterback Brian Sipe winning the AFC MVP award. In the first meeting of the teams that year, though, the Steelers were without Terry Bradshaw, Lynn Swann, Franco Harris, and John Stallworth because of injuries and lost a tight comeback game, 27-26. Though Pittsburgh was still 4-4 after that loss and just nine months removed from a Super Bowl win, there was sense that something had changed and the Steelers of the 1970s were no longer.*

Even the locals got that sense. "The once-proud Steeler defense was finally exposed as a shell of what it was in the glory years," The Pittsburgh Post-Gazette *reported in its game story. "That was the way the Steelers dynasty may have ended—under a howling crowd in Cleveland, with the swirling wind blowing paper around the stadium and the clouds darkening the scene as the final seconds ticked off. It couldn't have been a more symbolic setting for NFL Films to record their demise, with the voice of doom, John Facenda, droning in the background."*

WE HAD PLAYED them in Pittsburgh in 1978, and we played well. I missed a couple of long field goals. It went into overtime, we had the opening kickoff, and I can remember kicking the ball and I remember running down the field and Larry Anderson fumbled the ball. I saw it, the ball was on the ground, his knees weren't down, nothing. But the ball was on the ground and we recovered it on the 10-yard line or something like that. We were going to have the chance to win the game right there. But, one of the worst calls I have ever seen, they said, no, his knee was down. Well, even the film proved his knee was not down. They moved the ball into our territory, then they run a double-reverse flea-flicker kind of thing, a handoff to Bleier, then to Lynn Swann on a reverse, then back to Bradshaw and, touchdown. That was Bradshaw for you. If you gave him that chance, he was going to take advantage. It was the same thing in 1979, we went to overtime and lost in Pittsburgh. The Browns could never win at Three Rivers, it was not until something like 1986 that Cleveland won a game in that stadium.

But the turning point was 1980, I think not just for us but for the Steelers, too. That was sort of the start of that division becoming what it would be for years, really tough teams all around and

Pittsburgh was not quite as dominant anymore. On paper, we were not as good a team as teams like Houston and the Steelers, but we were pretty good, we were a young team and we were just really coming together. We started doing things in 1979 that made us think we had a pretty good team. In 1980, we started off 0-2, and after that second game, Coach Sam (Rutigliano) came in, and we could not believe we are 0-2. Sam comes in and says, 'Fellas, could you live with 14-0 the rest of the season?' We were like, sure, Sam. We lost three more games that year, we lost two games by three points each, and we lost one to Minnesota by five and we were winning that game late.

The big one was beating Pittsburgh, they were beaten up, but we were down late in the game (26-14 in the fourth quarter). Brian Sipe was so great that year, he brought us back and we beat them, 27-26, and that put us into a tie for first place. We were down, but Brian threw three touchdowns in the second half, and the funny thing was, all three came on the same play. 85 Halfback Option. We used our running backs as receivers out of the backfield a lot, guys like Calvin Hill, Greg Pruitt, Mike Pruitt, and that was a great play to go to, to take advantage of that. The Steelers had trouble stopping it.

One of the things that Coach Sam always talked about, in my last year, we beat them once, we should have beaten them twice. The thing that Coach Sam pointed out was that, how many Hall of Famers do we have from 1980? That would be two, Ozzie Newsome and Joe DeLamielleure. I think, not only their coach, but they had 10. Ten players who are in the Hall of Fame for the Steelers.

That sort of drove us to play a little harder. There was one game, I hit Franco Harris—he was young at the time, returning kicks, but he was still really, really strong. I hit Franco on a kickoff, and it was kind of a late hit. I got up looking for a flag, hoping I did not get called because I thought it was obvious I hit him hard and hurt him. But there was no flag and he just popped right up. I could not understand it, I hit him as hard as I could. That's just being a kicker though. Imagine, I am 195, and was a strong safety in college, so I knew how to hit. But against Franco Harris, didn't matter. His leg was as big as my body.

But I just remember, even when we were struggling, every bus trip we took to Pittsburgh, it was pretty quiet on that bus. The closer you got to Pittsburgh, the quieter the bus got. And unfortunately, when I was playing, forgive the terminology, but in the '70s, they kicked our butts just about every time we played them. We could never really beat them, especially not in Pittsburgh. It was the rivalry that had been. They were the Pukes-burgh Steelers, they would call them in Cleveland. It was a love-hate deal, only without the love. We didn't like them, they didn't like us. It just grew and grew and grew.

Key Rivalry Game:

December 13, 1981, at Three Rivers Stadium. Bengals 17, Steelers 10.

	1	2	3	4	OT	Final
Bengals	0	10	7	0		17
Steelers	0	3	0	7		10

Tom Dinkel

Linebacker

Team: Cincinnati Bengals, 1978-85

Tom Dinkel was drafted by the Bengals in 1978 out of Kansas, where, he says, he studied closely the style of play of fellow linebackers like Jack Ham and Jack Lambert. He wound up playing eight seasons in Cincinnati, which turned around its history against the Steelers at about the same time. In 1981, the Bengals swept the Steelers and took that momentum all the way to the Super Bowl.

THINGS WERE CHANGING by 1980, 1981. I would not say the Steelers were on their way down, but they had guys who had been there a long time and I think the rest of the division was catching up to them. We had Forrest Gregg that year, we had two great coordinators, Lindy Infante on the offensive side and Hank Bullough with us on the defense. They were so great at working with the personnel we had and getting the most out of us—we had talent, we just did not have the discipline we needed. That was what Forrest Gregg brought, he was from the Vince Lombardi school. When you were on Forrest Gregg's time, you were supposed to be working 100 percent of the time.

It's funny, the thing I remember most about that game actually was after the game. The Bengals never allowed us to have any beers or stuff on the plane afterward, that was one of Paul Brown's things. When I was a rookie, I was assigned by one of the veterans, I was in charge of contacting the visiting team's equipment manager to line up three or four cases of beer for after the game. I would collect five bucks or so from our guys after the game, and I would take the money to the visiting team's equipment manager—this guy's name was Iron Mike, of course—and he would always have these beers all iced down for us, and he would have a little spread with salami and some stuff like that in his little back room. I would have to keep track of who paid for what, but they took care of us in Pittsburgh. We would sit there and drink beers in Iron Mike's room, then get on the bus and finish off another one or two because it was a long ride to the airport. And I kept doing it after I was a rookie, because if I did it right, I would have enough money left over to pay for my airport parking when we got home to Cincinnati.

That game in 1981, I recall that game, Kenny (Anderson) had a bad toe or something wrong with his foot where he had to play with a steel plate in his shoe. He was not allowed to bend his foot that much. He was mobile, he took a lot of sacks, but Kenny was mobile. That game, he had to be on the move quite a bit. But he couldn't run too much so he would throw these little swing passes to Pete Johnson, and Johnson, we would call him the Runaway Beer Truck. When he hit you, that is what it felt like. And during that game, there were a few plays that Kenny made the swing pass to Pete and Jack Lambert was on him, and Pete went down and ran over Lambert. More than once. He didn't break the tackle, but he flattened Lambert as they both went down and got positive yards. That's the kind of thing that, if you're playing the Steelers and you see that, it gives you extra adrenaline. 'Pete just ran over Jack Lambert!'

That was the game we clinched the division for the first time. And it was good that I had the extra beers with me. I remember walking on the plane and I was sort of hiding a beer, which we were not supposed to have on the plane. But I put one on Forrest Gregg's lap while he was sitting there next to Paul Brown, he always sat next to him on the team plane. I said, 'Coach, I found this in the hallway, but I wanted to give it to you.' The best part was, those Iron City beers, they always had pictures of the Steelers team on them, so it was perfect. I said, 'Coach, congratulations, this is a great win.' He just said, 'Thank you, Thomas.' I don't think he ever called me Tom. Paul Brown sort of frowned. But it was cool.

We studied them a lot. We got to where we knew how they were going to run those inside traps. They were so good at the execution, but we were good at diagnosing those plays. I don't think Franco had too many good games against us. Once you get him running laterally, sideline to sideline, you're golden. If you give him a head of steam, you are in trouble. But if you can bounce the line, hit the backfield, penetrate, you could take him out of what he wants to do. But you have to deal with those big studs they have on the line, guys like Mike Webster and Jon Kolb double-teaming the nose tackle—we played the 3-4—and as a linebacker, you better step up and fill that gap and bounce Franco outside. That's what we started doing very well. All in all, we were well prepared against him. Fortunately, for me, I was catching him at the latter period of his career. But Franco wasn't a hard runner, he was not going to hurt you, but he had that deceptive speed where he is so smooth you can hardly tell how hard he is running.

The Steelers would tell you what they're doing. They were straightforward about it. They'd tip their hand but they did not care because they were the Steelers. If you played them, you were going to get the inside trap with Franco Harris, and over the years, we got better and better with our run defense and we were able to stop that play. But then you were going to get Bradshaw looking deep for those guys, Swann and Stallworth. Bradshaw was tough and he was a player, he was a great competitor. As Bengals players, we will always argue that Kenny Anderson should be in the Hall of Fame, when you look how he compares with Bradshaw, but Bradshaw had a team of Hall of Famers around him. But Terry was a player. There was one time, they were pushing toward the red zone, I came through on a blitz and he threw the ball, he was a very hard thrower. His hand hit my facemask and the sound was so loud, this '*Bing!*' and I thought, I swear to God he just broke his finger. I heard him cussing and ranting and raving, shaking his hand, and I thought maybe he would have some trouble. Next play, he throws a touchdown, of course. That was Bradshaw, he was just tough. He epitomized that team.

Ross Browner

Defensive Lineman

Team: Cincinnati Bengals, 1978–87

After four years as a starter on the defensive line at Notre Dame—where he won the Lombardi Trophy and the Outland Trophy as the nation's best lineman—Browner was chosen by Cincinnati with the eighth overall pick in 1978. As a native Ohioan, even before he played his first game, he had an understanding of what it meant to dislike the Steelers.

WHEN I FIRST got to the NFL, the question for us in Cincinnati was how were we ever supposed to get to the playoffs when we had the Pittsburgh Steelers in our division? They were the big bullies of the block, they were beating everybody. When I got to the Bengals, I had grown up in Warren, Ohio, so I always had a pretty good feeling for Ohio and I was happy I ended up on an Ohio team. Paul Brown was one of my mentors when I was coming out of high school because he came to our All-Star game in Ohio—Paul Brown was from Ohio, too—and came into the locker room. He said, 'What school are you going to, young man?' and I said, 'I am getting ready to go to Notre Dame.' He said that is a good school, and he said he would be watching me. I thought he was joking around, but when it came time for me to be drafted, Cincinnati was looking at me and I remembered Paul Brown saying he would be watching and that it would be good to go play for him for an Ohio team. Playing in the state of Ohio, we were all Cleveland Browns fans growing up so we knew all about disliking those Steelers.

At that time, it was developing into a great division, because you had the Oilers playing very well, the Browns were becoming a better team and we had put together a lot of young talent in Cincinnati. So I think that laid the groundwork for all the division battles you saw after that. But it was still all about Pittsburgh, they were the Super Bowl champions. I remember being on the field with those guys, whether it is Bradshaw or Franco Harris or Joe Greene, and you get star-struck. But I kept telling myself, 'They got to put their pants on one leg at a time, too.' You really had to get excited and up your game against them—they were so business-like, so professional. You might know some of the guys off the field, but you show up on game day and they're not there to have fun. It makes you become a better professional. They were the bullies, it was like going to the playground and seeing the big kid pushing everybody around. That was the Steelers. We played them two times a year, and during practice, we would all be shouting, 'Steeler week!' because we knew it would be special. You did not want to get out there and get your butt kicked.

When we beat them in Pittsburgh in that game, it gave us that confidence, and we took that all the way into the Super Bowl that year. Whenever you can beat a team that has so many champions, a team your organization has struggled to beat for so many years, it changes your mindset. That's the thing, you had Cleveland go to the Super Bowl, and we went to the Super Bowl the next year. That was not an accident. We went those times because if you were in that division with Pittsburgh, you had to lift up your game, because we had been trying to beat the Steelers for so many years we all developed into very good teams because of it.

They had an offensive tackle at that time, Larry Brown, he was very good and strong, good size, good technique. It took a lot to get around him, because you had to be strong, too, and you had to try to outthink him. The thing was, you could finally get by your man on their line, and Terry Bradshaw was just so hard to bring down. For one thing, he was strong, but more than that, he always seemed to know when you were coming, he had good awareness and he was very good at just giving you a side step so you would miss him. You could be right there ready to bring him down, but he would move just enough to give him room to get rid of the ball. He would flip right out of your hit and you would be grabbing at air. But I did sack him a couple of times, and he was funny about it. I'd bring him down and he would get up and look at me and say, 'Browner! I knew that was you!' He would crack me up. I have a picture of me in my trophy room, my rookie year, sacking Terry Bradshaw. That was a good moment for me, it made me think, 'OK, I belong in this league.'

Key Rivalry Game:

October 10, 1983, at Riverfront Stadium. Steelers 24, Bengals 14.

	1	2	3	4	OT	Final
Steelers	7	3	0	14		24
Bengals	0	14	0	0		14

The Steelers registered a record nine sacks on the Bengals, but it was one sack in particular that stood out. In the first quarter, with the ball deep in their own end, Bengals quarterback Kenny Anderson dropped back to pass, was chased down by defensive end Keith Gary and sacked. Gary grabbed Anderson by the face mask, though, twisting Anderson's helmet 180 degrees. Anderson first went to the turf as Gary celebrated and then went to Christ Hospital, where X-Rays found his neck had been sprained. After the game, Forrest Gregg told reporters, "We need rules to control this stuff. When a player acts maliciously, he should be ejected right then and there."

The Bengals led, 14-10 in the fourth quarter, but long interception returns by Ron Johnson and Harvey Clayton off Anderson's backup, Turk Schonert, helped the Steelers rally and move their record to 4-2. Pittsburgh would finish 10-6 in 1983, and win the Central Division for the first time since 1979.

Ross Browner

Browner, whose son, Max Starks, played for Pittsburgh, found Gary's play on Anderson to be unusual in a rivalry that could be rough, but not dirty.

THAT WAS NOT professional or classy from the Steelers team, that was not something that we looked at like it was how you expected Pittsburgh to play. The player (Gary), he not only made the tackle, but then he sort of celebrated while our quarterback was lying there. That was a game I would have liked to win and we felt like our defense did a good job on them, we had put ourselves into a position to win. They were tough, they were going to use all the tricks of the trade, but they were not really dirty. We would try to beat the snot out of each other, but we mostly kept it clean. So when that happened to Kenny, it really put a bad taste in your mouth to have that happen. We had a lot of friends on those teams, and we were not friends on the field, but we would not expect to have them take a cheap shot.

Tom Dinkel

Though the Steelers had knocked out Anderson even before the 1983 game, when he was clotheslined by safety Glen Edwards in 1974 and remained on the turf for five minutes, Anderson actually had a special fondness for the Steelers. And despite the vitriol aimed at Gary for his face mask, Dinkel understood his point of view.

I **NEVER THOUGHT THEY** were dirty players, I just thought they were damn good, damn tough players. Everybody today thinks a rivalry is about fistfights and cheap shots and all this verbiage. It's not. It's just, OK, you beat my ass this play. Now I have got to beat you. It was tough football in the AFC Central in those days.

But 1983, Kenny got his neck rung by Keith Gary. Believe it or not, I think the play itself was a total accident. I say that because three or four weeks later, I got a fine from the NFL when I got called for a face mask on Greg Pruitt of the Cleveland Browns. I had maybe two fingers on the face mask but I got a $1,000 fine because it just looked bad and his head turned. I appealed it, we had different angles on the play, I was trying to show it was not malicious. But in the midst of the NFL's defense of the fine, they show the Keith Gary footage, him ripping Kenny Anderson's head off. And Rozelle said, 'Keith Gary tried to use that same defense, that he was off balance and just reaching.' So I could understand it from Keith's perspective. I think the newspaper photos that came out about it made it look pretty bad. There is a great one of Kenny, and you can see the front of his jersey and you can see the back of his helmet on his head above it, his head is doing a total *Exorcist* thing. It took Kenny out of the game, and that was the game where they did not even score an offensive touchdown and they beat us, 24-14. They had nine first downs the whole game, we shut them down. But they scored three defensive touchdowns.

Kenny loved those guys. They roughed him up a lot over the years, but that was just football, it is not like now where every play with the Steelers and Bengals turns into a fight. Every game in Pittsburgh, someone would have to go fetch Kenny Anderson, we would have to drag him out of their locker room. It would be like, 'Come on Kenny, bus is leaving.' One time, he did not make the bus. He ended up riding to the airport on the equipment truck because he was hanging out in their locker room and the team bus already left. The equipment truck was last to leave for the airport so he had to hop on that. If you could not find Kenny after a game in Pittsburgh, he was probably sitting in the sauna with the Steelers, drinking some Iron City beer. All those guys, they were great guys—it was a bitter rivalry, even though we were not a good team in the late '70s, we were playing for pride, and that is what a good rivalry is all about.

We tried to emulate them. When Forrest Gregg took over the Bengals, he brought in a coordinator, Hank Bullough, and of course, Bullough brought in Dick LeBeau, Dick Modzelewski as our defensive line coach. We just got to learn how to study the Steelers so closely. Hank was one of those classroom freaks who just wanted to study film over and over and over. But the great thing about Steeler week is we would watch their defense on film, so you got the chance to study what their defense was doing. Jack Lambert, Andy Russell, Jack Ham—for me and the other linebackers, we wanted to watch those guys play, we spent as much time studying what they were doing as we did the offense. Just how they played the game.

Ham was so versatile and skilled, and Andy Russell was just perfect with his technique and then you had Lambert who would hit anything that moved. For me, to watch Jack Ham play the linebacker position, his techniques were so fundamentally perfect. He was a slow white guy like me, and if that is where you're starting, you better have perfect technique because you have got to buy time and save steps. If you are lining up against Bennie Cunningham, they listed him at 250, but I swear the guy was 280, 290, because he was 6-5 and huge. But he was standing next to Larry Brown, who is 6-4 and 300 pounds, and he was next to Steve Courson or Jon Kolb and they were huge. They were all huge. So you had to be quick and smart and really, you had to have great technique to beat guys like that. It was total respect for those Steelers players.

Key Rivalry Game:

November 4, 1984, at Three Rivers Stadium. Steelers 35, Oilers 7.

	7	2	3	4	OT	Final
Steelers	7	14	14	0		35
Oilers	0	0	7	0		7

After a long, wet slog of a game, Steelers beat reporter John Adams wrote, "If you must spend a Sunday afternoon in the rain, spend it with the Houston Oilers—the National Football League's best umbrella." It was a fitting line following a game in which the Steelers poured five touchdowns on hapless and winless (0-10) Houston, which fumbled four times and allowed quarterback Warren Moon to be sacked five times. The Steelers went to 6-4 and took control of the Central Division, which they would go on to win again in 1984, advancing to the AFC Championship game.

But while the Steelers were trouncing the Oilers, one Houston assistant coach was watching from the press box, seething. The blowout made a special impression on defensive coordinator Jerry Glanville.

Jerry Glanville

Coach

Teams: Houston Oilers, 1985-89; Atlanta Falcons, 1990-93

Jerry Glanville had been coaching in college when he made the jump to the NFL in 1974 and eventually worked his way up to defensive coordinator for the Falcons from 1978 to 1982. He was with the Bills in 1983 before taking the defensive coordinator's role on Hugh Campbell's staff in Houston in 1984.

I WENT TO HOUSTON as an assistant in 1984, and I really did not know the history. But we went and played in Pittsburgh in maybe the tenth week of the year. We had not won a game. They came out and they just killed us, like maybe 35-0 or 35-7. I was in the press box and after the game, I rode the elevator down with a guy on the Pittsburgh staff, Tony Dungy. He was their defensive coordinator. It felt like they had just beaten us by 50. They were sacking us every play, killing Warren Moon, turning him upside down on every play. We were so stupid we were still trying to throw the ball, and they were making us pay for it every time. Poor Warren Moon was trying to keep playing, and there was Tony Dungy, calling a blitz on every play, knocking him down, putting him on that hard turf.

I was riding the elevator down and looking at Tony Dungy and I thought, someday the shoe would be on the other foot. I said to myself, 'Pittsburgh, they just mistreated us. If I ever get to be a head coach, I am not going to let any team mistreat you, like they mistreated us.' So when I became the head coach, I didn't realize that the Oilers and the great Bum Phillips, one of the greatest coaches ever, they had never won a game in Pittsburgh. They were 0-26, how about that? 0-26. We were fortunate enough to change that, and we drove poor Chuck Noll crazy—we never lost in Pittsburgh.

I coached one year in Buffalo, and my wife was tired of the snow up to the dining room window every day. So I had two interviews for jobs, one in Pittsburgh and one in Houston. Chuck offered me the job, but I told him I think I was going to go with Houston. He said, 'You go there. You go there. You look over at me, twice a year, and I will smile because we'll be kicking your butts twice a year.' He didn't say butt, though. I went there, and he was right. When I was an assistant in Houston, they did not just beat us, they mauled us. He beat us so bad, if it had been a heavyweight fight they would have called it in the fourth round. Sitting through that, I decided if I was going to be a head coach, I would not let my team have that happen to them.

Warren Moon

Quarterback

Teams: Houston Oilers, 1984-93; Minnesota Vikings, 1994-96; Seattle Seahawks, 1997-98; Kansas City Chiefs, 1999-2000

After he could not get signed by an NFL team despite an outstanding senior season at the University of Washington, Warren Moon starred for six seasons in the Canadian Football League, winning five championships and a league MVP award. When he was ready to move to the NFL in 1984, Houston won the bidding. Moon played for the Oilers until 1994 and played seven more seasons with the Vikings, Seahawks, and Chiefs. He was inducted into the Hall of Fame in 2006. In that 1984 loss in Pittsburgh, he was 10-for-20 passing with 133 yards.

I **FACED THE STEELERS** more than any other team I faced in my career, even after I left Houston, I faced them in Minnesota and in Seattle, too, going to Pittsburgh. But even from the beginning, the thing that stands out is just that physical toughness, you knew if you were playing the Steelers, you better pull your chinstrap a little bit tighter that weekend. It was going to be a physical ballgame. For me, as the one throwing the football, it was going to be especially tough because they were known for getting after the quarterback. You knew they were going to be relentless with that. That game in Pittsburgh was my first year in the NFL, and I just remember being surprised by how much that team blitzed and how good they were at it. I took a lot of hits.

Probably the worst hit around that time was one of the first times I played them, early in my career (1985), and back then I used to try to run around a little bit. I remember I went back to pass and I ran out of the pocket, a couple of their big linemen got in the backfield so I scrambled out and I was running down the sideline at the Astrodome. I was trying to tiptoe down the sideline and get a couple of extra yards on a scramble. Their safety, Donnie Shell, came across the field and he hit me so hard, he gave me a hip pointer and I had to leave the game. From that day on, I knew that I had to really be selective about running around in the National Football League. I couldn't run around like I did in Canada. I was definitely more of a passer after I took that hit from Donnie Shell. That made me learn a few things about just getting out of bounds.

Key Rivalry Game:

December 16, 1984, at Los Angeles Memorial Coliseum. Steelers 13, Raiders 7.

	1	2	3	4	OT	Final
Steelers	3	0	0	10		13
Raiders	0	0	0	7		7

No, the Raiders were not an AFC Central rival. But this game had enormous meaning for the new coach of the Cincinnati Bengals, Sam Wyche. Pittsburgh entered the final week of the year 8-7, while the Bengals were 7-8. Cincinnati closed with Buffalo, then 2-13, at home, and the Steelers had to go across the continent to play the 11-4 Raiders. If all went as planned for Wyche, the Bengals would wind up 8-8 with a win in the early game, and the Steelers would fall to 8-8, too, putting Cincinnati into the playoffs. But the Raiders could muster just 188 yards on the day, and things just did not go according to Wyche's plan.

Sam Wyche

Coach Teams: Cincinnati Bengals, 1984-91; Tampa Bay Bucaneeers, 1992-95

Sam Wyche had been on the staff of Bill Walsh in 1981 when the 49ers won Super Bowl XVI behind Joe Montana. He moved on to coach Indiana for one season before getting the head-coaching job in Cincinnati, where he led a remarkable Bengals turnaround.

MY FIRST YEAR in Cincinnati was 1984, and we started that year, we were 0-5, but we went 8-3 from there and we were really getting some attention in Cincinnati, which was a good thing, of course. We played Buffalo and won the game and finished 8-8, and we had a chance to win that division even with a .500 record. So we win the game, and we have all the television affiliates—ABC, NBC, CBS—in Cincinnati over to my house after the game so we can watch the Pittsburgh game. I was thinking fate is on our side, we turned this thing around, we're going to the playoffs. They were 8-7 and they just needed to lose that game and we would tie for the division, we had the tiebreaker, so we would go to the playoffs.

Now, the Steelers are in Oakland, and the Raiders are just about 7-point favorites. Oakland was a really good team that year,

Marcus Allen, Jim Plunkett, a really good team. So we figure it is in the bag. We have the media there, we are feeding them and all, we were thinking this will be good publicity for the team going into the play-offs, get people excited. We watch that game and what do you know, the Steelers defense plays great, it's 3-0 most of the game. It's 10-0. It's 13-0. And the Steelers go on and win, and we go from having a play-off celebration to now I have to go to the cameras and be entertaining and say something pithy wishing Pittsburgh well and representing the division. I had to put on a different face really quickly. That was my introduction to the Steelers and the AFC Central.

Key Rivalry game:

October 25, 1987, at Three Rivers Stadium. Steelers 23, Bengals 20.

	1	2	3	4	OT	Final
Steelers	3	0	7	13		23
Bengals	7	7	6	0		20

After a strong 10-6 performance in 1986, the Bengals got off to a rocky start in 1987, but the possibility of a turnaround looked promising in the first half in Pittsburgh, as the Bengals led, 14-3, and carried a 20-10 lead into the fourth quarter. Steeler fans had turned on quarterback Mark Malone, who was six-for-15 for 53 yards in the first half and heard what one reporter called "deafening" boos when he returned from the locker room. But Malone led a fourth-quarter rally, the Steelers scoring 13 unanswered points.

The Bengals, though, still had a chance. Gary Anderson put the Steelers in the lead with a field-goal at 1:51, but when Cincinnati got the ball back, quarterback Boomer Esiason moved the offense to the Steeler 33-yard line with 18 seconds left and no timeouts, then completed another pass to Mike Martin, who was tackled without going out of bounds. Rather than set up for a spike to stop the clock, Bengals coach Sam Wyche sent on the field-goal unit as the clock wound down. By the time kicker Jim Breech was set up to attempt a tying try, time ran out. After the game, Steelers assistant Dick Hoak shrugged and said, "Wicky Wacky Wyche screws up again."

Sam Wyche

The Bengals went just 4-11 in 1987, and certainly, some of their foibles fall to Wyche. But when it came to the kick that never happened in Pittsburgh, he at least had a reason.

WE WERE PLAYING Pittsburgh and the game is real close. We're down by three, it is third down and a few yards. We complete a pass and the receiver falls forward and there are just seconds left on the clock. We don't have any time-outs at this point. When we snapped the ball on the previous play, there were 18 or 20 seconds left, so we have to hurry. If we made the first down, we were going to stop it and clock it that way. If he didn't make the first down, you couldn't clock it because it was fourth down and now you're turning the ball over.

So the pass is complete, and I was yelling in the headset to Bruce Coslet in the booth, asking him, is it a first down? He was saying he didn't know, it was close. We were waiting on the ref to make the signal, but we did not have time so I decided, I better get the field-goal team out there as quick as I can. We could not afford to wait. We were a second-and-a-half late kicking the ball. We lost the game, 23-20, and well, I took a lot of criticism for that. Their line coach Dick Hoak said something to the reporters on the way down the elevator, he said, 'That's Wicky Wacky Wyche for you.' That was where my nickname came from—it's pronounced WYSHE, not WYK-EE, but I guess his way sounds better. He thought we blew the call, but we blew the call because the officials did not give us the signal fast enough so we were not sure if we had the first down or not. I reported it to the league, and the league agreed with me, the refs should have stopped the clock to set the ball and signal first down or not.

Key Rivalry game:

December 20, 1987, at the Astrodome. Oilers 24, Steelers 16.

	1	2	3	4	OT	Final
Oilers	0	10	7	7		24
Steelers	3	3	7	3		16

The Handshake Game. On the field, the action had been rough. A fight during the game led to the ejection of three players, Oilers Richard Byrd and Doug Smith, and Steeler Frank Pollard, and Chuck Noll was so irritated by Houston's physicality he reportedly told one Oilers player, "Me and your coach on the sidelines right now. Who would win?" That Oilers coach was now Jerry Glanville, and though Noll refrained from going after Glanville during the game, he met him at midfield after the game and took his hand in a decidedly awkward and extended handshake. It was then that Noll gave Glanville a lecture that was broadcast around the country on video and in photos. Noll's exact wording is fuzzy, but it was reported in the next day's newspapers as: "If you send players after our players like that, I'll come after you. Don't forget that."

That set off weeks of sniping between the two organizations, and Glanville put together clips of seven hits he thought were dirty in that game, six by the Steelers. Noll said, "If you've got a true fight, that's one thing. But if you start one, that looks like it's being done purposely. They should have lost three or four players. Maybe the coach, too." But Houston center Jay Pennison said it was actually the

Steelers initiating trouble: "They were doing that to us the whole game. Evidently their game plan was to talk sh— to us and start fights."

Jerry Glanville

Glanville was promoted to head coach of the Oilers during the 1985 season, and he carried the lessons of that 35-7 loss in Pittsburgh with him. He not only tried to add swagger and toughness to his team, initiating what was known as the "House of Pain" at the Astrodome, but he took on a bad-guy persona. Glanville would typically be seen dressed completely in black, preferred black cowboy hats, and was known to ride a black motorcycle. While he became an archenemy of the Steelers, he actually saw his coaching style as an homage to the way Noll's teams played. Glanville's Oilers made the playoffs that year and won their first postseason game since 1979.

WE BEAT THEM twice in one year, up there and then down at our place. That was when old Chuck fell in love with my hand after the game. We had won, we beat them twice, they actually had players kicked out of that game, but somehow it was all my fault. I went to shake his hand and he grabs it and starts pointing at me. He was screaming, 'I can't wait to get you at our place, you'll pay for this. You'll pay for this when you come to our place.' I respected him and I treated him with the authority and dignity he should be treated with. I said, 'OK, we'll be there, good luck to you.' They showed that on TV for 10 days. I was proud of myself, I did not come back at him. I did not raise my voice or make any predictions. The first game after that, the next season, when they were going to get their revenge, it was the worst beating we ever gave them up there. We won by 20-something points (the final in that game was 34-14). We beat them to death. He didn't say anything after that. But I always respected him because he was a great competitor and his teams were so tough.

Pittsburgh was the focus. They had to be. In training camp—you might not believe this, I never told anybody this, but it is true—every Wednesday in training camp was Pittsburgh Day. We practiced against Pittsburgh during two-a-days, every Wednesday. Let me tell you, the practice was a bloodbath, because that's what you had to do to go up there and win. They could never figure out what happened, because all the sudden a team that could never win up there, we won up there and won up there and won up there. What they did not know is we were playing against them every week in training camp, so our guys were really, really focused on those games. I knew that to change the temperament of those games, so we were not getting mistreated, we had to change the way we were playing them. Whatever we were doing was not working. So let's change. In the first practice, we would line up defensively while our offense ran Pittsburgh's plays. The other half, our defense would run Pittsburgh's defense. So half the day, we were running against their offense, half the day we were against their defense. Every Wednesday. The players didn't like it. We were in San Antonio, and it was hot enough to fry an egg on the sidewalk. So when we got to Pittsburgh, the guys, they were already mad as hell.

We beat Pittsburgh one year in Pittsburgh (in 1989), we were a dome team, but we beat them in an all-out blizzard. We had a guy named Lorenzo White, our running back. It was snowing so bad that nobody could stand up, it was so slippery. But Lorenzo White, I drafted him out of Michigan State, he wore a 15-AAA shoe. I had him run a toss sweep and everybody else was slipping and falling but Lorenzo, his feet were so big it looked like he had on snowshoes. He went on in there for the winning touchdown, in a blizzard. It was the only time I have seen in Pittsburgh that most of the crowd did not show up. That's how bad it was. Whiteout blizzard, that is the only way you were going to keep Pittsburgh fans from coming to the game.

I thought the only way to beat them was to be just like them. Warren Moon got mad at me one time when we were playing the Steelers. I decided we were going to go out and just not pass the ball to start the game. We were not going to pass for a long, long time. I think we ran 23 plays, we were just handing off the ball, going right at them, playing their game. Warren said, 'When are we going to throw the ball?' I said, 'We will throw when that defense gives up.' He goes, 'That's the Pittsburgh Steelers, they ain't never going to give up.' But the first pass we threw was a touchdown, about the middle of the second quarter. But that was the thing—you could not go in there and play Frisbee. They were going to beat you silly if you are not going to go in there and play just as tough as they do. You better not go in there with your new pads on. You better go in there with the philosophy that you are going to break a few noses or you are not going to come out alive. He caused us to change our philosophy.

We had an assistant coach named Doug Shively, and he was being interviewed and he was asked, what is it between the Pittsburgh Steelers and the Oilers? He said that Jerry respects Chuck so much and loves so much the way they play the game, that we decided we were going to play just like them. And he was right. We enjoyed that. I am not sure the people of Pittsburgh appreciated that. But if you are going to win, if you are going to beat 'em, you better bring your big-boy pants with you. That was the way we approached it. We would call it straight-ahead-running, no-fear-dodging. When we played Pittsburgh, I would tell my running backs, if you run out of bounds, I am benching you. You're not playing anymore. Not against everybody. But against Pittsburgh, you hit the boundary and you don't step out, you turn back in and put your shoulder down. The only way they'll respect you, you have got to run right at a Pittsburgh Steelers linebacker or DB, whoever is coming at you. That was the only way you could play the game against them. We had been 0-26 in Pittsburgh. Well, that's how you change 0-26.

Ray Childress

Defensive Lineman

Teams: Houston Oilers, 1985-95; Dallas Cowboys, 1996

Ray Childress was a five-time Pro Bowl defensive end who was chosen with the third pick in the draft in 1985. He became emblematic of the rise of the Oilers defense in the late 1980s and early '90s and played better against the Steelers in his career—12.5 sacks—than any other team.

THEY WERE A big division rivalry, and all of the teams in our division were good ones. It was a tough division. We always wanted to play well against those guys. But for me, it was respect. That had a lot to do with it, when I played or prepared against the Steelers. You knew the history of the Steelers and all the things they accomplished, you knew they were going to be disciplined and well coached. They were going to be really physical, a tough team. They had that culture of the tough steel-town type of team, that character. We faced them a lot, and we had some good battles against them. My anticipation was that you were going to be in for a fight.

The thing with Chuck Noll and Jerry, I think that only fired the players up, at least on the defensive side. We didn't know what was happening as it was going on because we were just going to the locker room, but after the game, we all saw it. Chuck Noll kind of scolded Jerry Glanville on his behavior. Maybe he deserved it but we didn't care. It fired us up in the locker room. We were just trying to do some of the things they did. Jerry Glanville liked to have all-out blitzes and some really off-the-wall coverages, blitzes, all kinds of things. I remember Noll scolding him and I think Noll just didn't like him. He wore all black, he left the tickets for Elvis Presley at the will-call windows, that kind of stuff. I think Noll was more old-school. But I don't think Jerry really cared.

Key Rivalry game:

December 31, 1989, at the Astrodome. Steelers 26, Oilers 23 (OT).

	1	2	3	4	OT	Final
Steelers	7	3	3	10	3	26
Oilers	0	6	3	14		23

The Steelers were seven-point underdogs traveling to Houston on New Year's Eve for a wild-card playoff game and were largely dominated by the Oilers, who outgained Pittsburgh, 380 yards to 289. Warren Moon was outstanding, throwing for 315 yards and two touchdowns, both going to Ernest Givins, who had 11 catches and 136 yards, mostly against untested rookie cornerback Carnell Lake. But for all the Houston dominance, the Oilers failed to push into the end zone and came out of the third quarter with just nine points. But after Moon completed his second touchdown in the fourth quarter, the Oilers took a 23-16 lead with six minutes to play. Quarterback Bubby Brister responded with an 82-yard drive that lasted more than five minutes, tying the game and setting up overtime. The situation there quickly turned grim for the Steelers when a poor punt gave the Oilers great field position at the Pittsburgh 45. But when Moon handed off to Lorenzo White on a sweep, cornerback Rod Woodson lasered to him and stuck White behind the line of scrimmage, with linebacker Tim Johnson coming in to help dislodge the ball from White for a fumble, which Woodson recovered.

Shortly thereafter, when the Steelers drive stalled after five plays, Noll had a choice—should he attempt a 50-yard field goal, a distance from which kicker Gary Anderson had not tried all year, or punt to pin the Oilers inside the 20? He asked the opinion of defensive coordinator Rod Rust, who'd watched Moon carve out big chunks of yardage with passes all afternoon. Rust advised a kick. Anderson made it, and the Steelers advanced. It was Glanville's last game in Houston.

Warren Moon

Despite his big day, Moon was somber after the game, saying, "I hate to go out this way." But Houston's prospects brightened shortly thereafter—in 1991, the Oilers won the AFC Central for the first time since 1967 and did so again in 1993. The Steelers remained a prime rival, though, especially Rod Woodson, the guy so critical to Pittsburgh's 1989 playoff win.

THAT WAS A tough loss, because that year, we had a really good team. We moved the ball a lot, but we just were not getting it into the end zone, so it was a close, close game all the way and we took a lead in the fourth quarter but they tied it up. Then in overtime, Rod Woodson just does what he always did which was make big plays.

That was a physical game, every time we played them it was physical. But you have to remember, there were a lot of things Jerry Glanville did as a coach that I disagreed with, to be honest with you. He changed the culture of that team, and that was good. But, especially that House of Pain stuff because that did as much to go against me as it did the other team. I got more physical play from it than the other teams got because other teams wanted to show our team they were more physical, and when they want to do that, they're going to hit the quarterback. You would play the Steelers who were always physical and we would be physical with them, but they would then take it out on me. I would get hit and guys would say, 'Welcome to our House of Pain.' Stuff like that. I took a lot of abuse because of it. Especially when you were throwing it as much as we were.

I think the Steelers kind of made Jerry who he was, or who he was trying to be. I think when he was going through the whole black thing, wearing black, trying to be intimidating like the Steelers—he never thought our Columbia blue uniforms were very intimidating.

Neither did I really, I thought it was a good-looking uniform but it definitely didn't scare the pants off people when we came out of the tunnel. I think he liked the fact that when the Steelers came out of the tunnel, they were intimidating right away and he wanted that for us. Whether they were good or not, you really didn't know until you lined up against them. In the tunnel, coming out, they sure looked intimidating. But Jerry's thing was always to try to be more physical than the Steelers. That was his thing. That was why he came up with that whole House of Pain crap, and he wore all black and rode around on a black motorcycle. He was infatuated with black. Even when he went to Atlanta, he changed their colors so that they would be more predominantly black. It just became his identity.

Rod Rust

As an assistant coach with Philadelphia, Kansas City, and New England, Rust had spent much of his career coaching against Noll. But in 1989, Rust signed on to be Noll's defensive coordinator. He was only there a year before returning to the Patriots as head coach, but he had an impact, working with Rod Woodson—who was in his third year—and installing an innovative coverage scheme. Of course, after Pittsburgh started 0-2, losing to Cleveland and Cincinnati by a combined score of 92-10, Rust did not think he would make it to Week 3 with the Steelers. But Noll had faith, and, capped by the playoff win in Houston, the Steelers made a remarkable turnaround.

THAT GAME, IT was overtime, we had tied up the game in the fourth quarter. We had a long drive, 80-something yards to go and tie up that game and get it to overtime. We were big underdogs,

Houston had been a preseason favorite, everyone thought they were going to the Super Bowl. But we had a pretty good idea how to play Houston, they would line up in an I-formation on first and second down, then run-and-shoot on third down, and they ran pretty much the same basic pattern—something Bill Walsh made popular in San Francisco—the tight end hooks, the wide receiver runs a real speed curl right about the numbers, the near back runs a flare out to the flat and the X receiver runs a lazy post. Warren Moon was so good, they could make that work, and I always thought they could have done so much more with that offense, we knew how to stop that pattern though. But we played them pretty well.

They had the ball in our territory early in the overtime. It looked like that was going to be the game. But Rod Woodson, he was an incomparable football player, really a great, great player, and a great person, too. They threw a toss out to their running back (Lorenzo White) and Rod came in, and our linebacker, Tim Johnson was in there, too, but Rod made a phenomenal play. He tackled him with one arm and forced a fumble with the other arm, he stripped it right out and we got a turnover. Rod ran it back maybe to their 45-yard line or so. Our offense, we got a first down but that was it, so it would be a 50-yard kick.

Chuck said something about punting and keeping them deep, and I said, with their offense, we can't promise to keep them down there. That was the run-and-shoot, Warren Moon and those receivers. One 30-yard pass and they are right back here anyway, and your punt is erased. He asked me if we should kick it deep and pin them down. I just said, I can't promise you we will keep them there. Gary Anderson was our kicker, so I told Chuck, let's give him a chance. He went out there and he made it. A writer later wrote that I said I told Chuck we could not stop the Oilers anyway so we might as well kick it. But that is not really right. I thought we could stop them from scoring. I just did not see an advantage in punting because with that Houston offense, they could pick up 30 yards in one play.

We won the game, and if it were not for John Elway the next week in Denver, we might have gone to the Super Bowl. That was really a big swing considering the way we started. I was persona non grata the first two weeks. With good reason. The first week, actually, it was not as bad defensively as it was the second week. The first week, we lost 51-0 but it was 17-0 before the defense even really took the field, they returned two fumbles for touchdowns. It was not a pretty start for us. The second week was bad, and that was one where we could not stop them, Cincinnati. It was 41-10 and we could not stop them, we gave up 500 yards.

I was trying to put in my system, the way I wanted them to play and the players were just having a hard time with it. It was 4-deep coverage, I invented it, but it requires that players spend a lot of time studying and understanding how to make decisions on the field. They were struggling with it. It was a new thing at the time, it was an unknown entity. Chuck came to see me on Monday night after that second game, I was up in my office, and I told him, 'Coach, I believe in what we are doing, but I apologize for the way we're playing. I can't prove it to you right now. If you want me to change something, tell me and I will change it.' I hated saying that because I believed in what we were doing. He looked at me and thought for a moment, and he said, 'Coach what you know.' Any time you get out on a limb with a new system, you don't know if it is going to be validated. Chuck could have stopped it right there. But he supported me. The next week, we simplified things, we shut out Minnesota in the second half and won the game. That team was 0-2 and in a bad way, but we finished and went 9-7, made the playoffs.

SECTION 5

CHANGES

CHAPTER 12

EXIT THE CHIEF

In 1988, the Steelers, perhaps the most stable organization in all of Americans sports at the time, were met with a sad shock: at 87 years old, Art Rooney suffered a stroke at—where else?—his office at Three Rivers Stadium and died at Mercy Hospital in Pittsburgh the next day. Upon his death, NFL Commissioner Pete Rozelle said, "He was a man who belonged to the entire world of sports. It is questionable whether any sports figure was more universally loved and respected."

Rozelle was not overstating the case. There are few, if any, members of the pro football owners' club who drew quite as much adulation and respect as Art Rooney, the fellow nicknamed the Chief, who owned and ran the Steelers almost as a side interest when he bought the team in 1933. Horse racing was Rooney's breadwinner, and legend had it that in one especially blessed two-day span at the track at Saratoga, N.Y., in 1938, Rooney cleared nearly $300,000, then returned home to tell his young pregnant wife, Kathleen, "We don't have to worry about money again."

Always chomping on a cigar and forever holding forth with whatever audience was handy—his clan hailed from County Down in Ireland, each member touched with the gift of gab—Rooney was a lovable character who knew how to keep things running smoothly within his own franchise while always respecting and looking out for his competitors around the NFL. When the Steelers won their first Super Bowl in 1975, the players gave Rooney the game ball, and Chuck Noll refused to accept the championship trophy from commissioner Pete Rozelle. He insisted Rooney do the honors.

With typical humility, he told the *Pittsburgh Post-Gazette*, "I guess they just wanted me to be a big shot for the day."

Rooney saw his football team go from pariah to paradigm in his last two decades at the helm and took great pride not only in the four Super Bowls the Steelers won in the 1970s, but in the roles his sons played in running the franchise. Where the Chief made an impact all around the league with small and unexpected acts of kindness, Dan Rooney did much the same after his father's passing. There is no shortage of stories about the Rooneys' fair and equitable treatment of players and coaches around the league.

Dick Vermeil

Coach

Teams: Philadelphia Eagles, 1976-82; St. Louis Rams, 1997-99; Kansas City Chiefs, 2001-05

Dick Vermeil was just thirty-five when he served as the offensive coordinator for the L.A. Rams in 1971. In the final game of the season, the Rams traveled across the country to play the Steelers on a day with a wind-chill temperature of just 16 degrees. His team, which finished 8-5-1 that year, was up, 16-7, at halftime when Vermeil got a visitor.

IF ANYONE MENTIONS the Pittsburgh Steelers, I think first of Art Rooney. The first time I met Mr. Rooney personally, I was the offensive coordinator for the Los Angeles Rams, I think in 1971. We were playing them in the last game of the season, in Pittsburgh. It was cold. It was windy. It was sort of what you expect for a December game at Three Rivers Stadium, if you know what I mean. Before the end of the first half, I was in the press box and it was cold in there, where our box was, and I was sitting there and halftime was coming and Mr. Rooney walked into the coordinator's box. He brought me a hot bowl of soup. I am serious now. There's not a lot of times as a coordinator that you will want someone coming into the box during a game, let alone the owner of the other team. But he sat down and told me about the soup, how it was made, saying, 'It is sure nice having you in Pittsburgh, hope you're enjoying your coaching career, you're young, you have a bright future,' all of that kind of thing. Here I am, it was 1971, and now 45 years later, I have not forgotten that story, that interaction. I have forgotten what I had for lunch yesterday, but I have not forgotten that story.

Lee Calland

On a young and rebuilding team in the early 1970s, Calland was a relatively grizzled veteran who had been with four organizations previously. As it turned out, he was the perfect candidate for a friendship with team owner Art Rooney. If his haggling with Steelers brass over contracts was not always easy, he got a much different view on negotiations when he left Pittsburgh for Oakland and owner Al Davis.

THE WHOLE ORGANIZATION was a great organization. There were young guys and there were old guys, there was a tradition there, the Chief, he would really take an interest in you as a person. Shoot, the Chief would take me out after practice, when we were in Latrobe for training camp doing two-a-days, we would get a break for lunch. And the Chief would take me aside and start talking with me, we would go to a tree and sit there right in front of the dorms, and he would share life with me. How life really was. Not just football, but real-life situations. So you got to feel like he was your family. The only problem is, you would talk with him so long, sometimes you would miss your lunch. That was the one trick, you had to make sure you got your lunch in when you were talking to the Chief. He had an interest in all the people in the organization beyond just football. He was a great guy, and he explained how things went. Not everyone could make star salaries, but everyone could make enough to take care of their families.

I used to argue about money a lot with his son. His son handled all the money, so he was the one I had to get into it with. But I always saw it like, you can fight and bicker with your family members, say what you wanted to inside the house, but once you got outside the house, in public, everything is OK. Keep it behind closed doors. We had some hellacious arguments about money, but that was his job. My job was to try to get as much money as I could. And he was tough. I remember the last time I talked with him about money, the last negotiation we had, I had intercepted seven passes the year before. I had a very good year. So we were going back and forth and—check this out now, tell this to the young guys playing now—we were talking about a $3,000 raise.

He said, 'If you make All-Pro, we will put the $3,000 in for next year.' I said, 'Whoa, first of all, I don't think you like me that much, and you have to push for me to get to the Pro Bowl before I can get there. So I think I would rather have that money now.' But it was family arguments, you know?

After 1972, they sent me out to the Oakland Raiders, and my first day out there, Al Davis came by and he was talking the talk, walking the walk, as you would expect. He is still one of the quickest guys I ever saw in my life, he could talk. He came by, dressed in white, white slippers, he was California all the way. I went to him and I said, 'Look Al, I need to talk to you about some money.' Three days later, I was gone. That was the difference.

Sam Wyche

Wyche had a tenuous relationship with just about all of the fan bases and coaching staffs for his AFC Central rivals (ask Cleveland Browns fans, or Houston Oilers coaches), but he did have a safe haven—in Pittsburgh, where the Rooneys were among Wyche's cohorts.

THE ROONEY FAMILY, they are some of my favorite people because you could always go and talk with them and they viewed everyone in the NFL as having a connection. I had my pilot's license and I used to like to fly in when I was coming to broadcast games after I was done with coaching. I would fly in and the first thing I would do was go into the owner's office and see Dan Rooney and let him know I made it OK, because the airfield in Pittsburgh was difficult, it had a little what they call an elbow break on the final approach into Pittsburgh, and if you are not really alert, you will miss the runway into Pittsburgh. He was an avid pilot. He had an A-36 Bonanza and I had a P-Baron twin-engine piston plane. So I would go in and we would talk flying, we would talk football, and then we would find something else to talk about, because with a game the next day, we didn't want to talk too much football. But it was always great to go in and spend time with them. We got to be good friends.

Bobby Ross

Ross had been dealing with the Steelers going back to his first pro coaching gig with Kansas City in 1978. But it was not until the 1994 AFC Championship game, when he was with the Chargers, that Ross had a breakthrough playoff win against Pittsburgh, a 17-13 win that sent

San Diego to the Super Bowl. After the game, Ross had an unexpected encounter with Dan Rooney.

IT WAS ONE of my big thrills, perhaps one of the biggest thrills I ever had in coaching, to win a playoff game in a place like Pittsburgh, which was always just the team you measured yourself against, going way back to when I started in the NFL in the '70s. After that game, I was the last one out of the locker room. I had to meet with the media, I had to talk with our coaches, I got in the shower, by myself, and they were waiting for me in the bus.

All of a sudden I hear somebody hollering out in the locker room, 'Coach Ross, Coach Ross!' I went to the end of the shower, and I poked my head out and there is Mr. Rooney. He had walked all the way down into our locker room, and there I am in the shower, but he sees me and he says, 'I just wanted to tell you, congratulations. That was a super win for your team. Best of luck in the Super Bowl.' That was the type of man he was. Great, great man, classy man. My image that I have of the Steelers is that the organization is very special, and it starts with him.

Bill Bergey

Bill Bergey was known as a big hitter, and during his seasons with the Bengals (1969-73), that made him many an enemy among Steeler fans. But in the 1980s, he was in the press box broadcasting Eagles games when he saw someone he wanted to meet.

AT ONE TIME, I was doing Eagles radio. I was doing the color commentary and we were in the radio booth at Three Rivers

Stadium, and I looked over in the next box and there was Art Rooney Sr. in there, chomping on a cigar. So I said to the play-by-play man, I asked him if I could have a minute, and I went over there to the next booth and I just said hello to Mr. Rooney. He was by himself, watching the game. So I sat with him and he was the coolest guy I think I ever met. It was such a pleasure to sit there and talk to him. I remember one time, I was told, he had walked into an owners' meeting with all the teams, and all the other owners stood up when he came in and gave him a standing ovation. He was really something. I thought that was so cool. He was such a classy guy, he took time with me, he was not one of those guys who said hi, hello, thanks and then expected to you to leave. He just rapped with me. He was a neat man.

Steve Grogan

The Patriots had not had a winning season in ten years when they went to Pittsburgh in Week 3 of the 1976 season, the year after Billy Sullivan had become the team's principal owner. Sullivan and his family long had ties to the Rooneys, through the Sullivan printing business, their involvement in football, and, of course, their strong ancestral ties. When the Patriots beat the Steelers, 30-27, under quarterback Steve Grogan, Sullivan got a reward from Rooney that he passed on to Grogan.

THAT WAS A huge game for our owner, Billy Sullivan. He was good friends with the Rooneys, he had been for a long time. You know, both Irish-Catholic families, they had known each other a long time. They were pretty friendly with each other and had business ties. It was a huge game for me, I started some games in my first year, but that was my first full year and we were a good team.

So after the game, I was happy. I talked to reporters and I was going to shower and all that. But Billy came into the locker room and handed me a cigar, a big cigar that Art Rooney had given to him as congratulations on the win. He just said, 'I want you to have it.' I put it in my bag, and I still have that cigar to this day, in a plastic bag. I don't think I will be smoking it, though. I knew it was a special thing. Mr. Rooney was known for his big cigars, so I knew I would be hanging onto that thing for a long time. I am afraid that now if I pick it up it will crumble to shreds, but I can say I still have it.

CHAPTER 13

"THIS IS A COACH YOU CAN PLAY FOR"

In late 1991, three years after the passing of owner Art Rooney, Steelers coach Chuck Noll strolled down a hallway in the team's offices at Three Rivers Stadium flanked by Dan Rooney, took a seat in a crowded interview room, and watched as Rooney read a statement beginning "Chuck Noll is retiring as the coach of the Steelers. It has been a wonderful 23 years. Chuck is a great man and he hasn't changed since Day One." While there was frequent discussion about his sometimes-rocky relationships with players—especially quarterback Terry Bradshaw—Noll was mostly hailed as a father figure by players. Even when it came to Bradshaw, who had a messy split with the Steelers while he tried to work through an injured elbow in 1983, when asked about the relationship at his retirement, Noll did something that might be considered surprising for any lifelong football coach but him: he quoted Emerson. "I heard somebody tell me poet Ralph Waldo Emerson probably put it best when he said, 'Your actions speak so loudly, I can't hear what you're saying,'" Noll said, indicating that the way Bradshaw had played for him during his career was more important than the things he said. "I'd like to keep it that way."

Over the course of his years running the Steelers, Noll earned a dual reputation as the taskmaster of football's toughest team on one hand, and as an affable mentor and friend on the other. While fans knew Noll as Emperor Chaz, stiff-lipped overseer of four

NFL champions, his players and colleagues knew a different guy altogether—approachable, self-deprecating, and always quick with advice, while also intellectually curious and well-versed on far-from-football topics like opera, sailing, piloting, and, of course, his beloved red wines.

Noll taught the Steelers the value of stability at the top. When Noll was hired in 1969, he was the 14th Steelers coach in the franchise's 35-year history. In the four decades that followed, Pittsburgh would have just three coaches: Noll, his replacement, Bill Cowher, and Mike Tomlin.

Lee Calland

Calland was brought to Pittsburgh in Noll's first season, after a brief stint in Chicago and six seasons split between the Vikings and Rams. Noll was trying to shore up a poor passing defense and wanted the help of a veteran defensive back.

THE FIRST THING that happened to me when I got to Pittsburgh is, I was coughing all over the place. I was cold. There was snow on the ground, the weather had just changed. I practiced with the team and I thought I was sick because after practice, I had this terrible cough in my throat. I thought maybe I was out of shape. Chuck came up to me after practice and said, 'Don't worry, it's just the change in climate.' I just looked at him funny and he smiled. I had just come from Chicago. He said cold weather is the best conditioning. He was a great guy, a great guy. A super coach, a super motivator, a super everything. We called him Charles.

When I got there, it was Charles's first year. We went 1-13, but you could see what he was doing. You could see he was building a team. There was a guy there who was a legend from the old team,

Chuck Hinton, he was a good defensive lineman. He was a legend when I got there. Chuck Noll really loved that guy, but he came into the locker room one day and addressed the team and he told us that he had to let him go—that was the 1970 season. He said it was one of the toughest decisions he had to make in his whole life. I knew the way he said it and the way it felt, he was not lying to us. It was really hard for him. But watching him do that, I felt like, this is a coach you can play for.

It was a little more segregated then. It was not like it is now, it was still segregated by races, the black players stuck around the black players and the white players and the Southern players and all of that. I was out with the guys one night, and I told all the guys, I said, 'Look, there's more talent here than our record says. We need to win for Chuck, because this guy has brought us all together, and if we don't win for him, we are going to wind up scattered all over the league and not have a chance to win a championship.' Because you could see, he was putting together a team that was going to be really good, but it was going to be up to the players and we had to make sure we trusted each other. Because Chuck could coach. So I just felt that, all we needed was not to take the games as just games to be played. We had to take it as the last game you were ever going to play in your life. It started getting better.

Red Miller

Miller had seen the Steelers plenty of times during his seventeen years as an assistant coach in the AFL and NFL, but it wasn't until he became head coach of the Broncos in 1977 that Miller really got a good sense for how hard and frustrating the Pittsburgh defense could be—or how soft and likable their coach could be.

COACH NOLL, WE called him Knowledge Noll, and it fit because he was such a good coach. His teams were always going to play the same way, he was not going to use gimmicks or tricks, you had to play straight-up football in order to beat him. We had some success against him, but he certainly had his success against us. They were not fancy. They played football, real football. Steelers football was hard play, all game, all 60 minutes. You had to coach that into your players.

I was with a few teams before I got to be a head coach—New England Patriots, Buffalo—and it seemed like every year, no matter what the team, you had to deal with Pittsburgh. But I got to know Chuck Noll over time, we would talk after our games, he was a very smart guy. You don't get to where he was unless you know what you are doing, and he knew what he was doing. The things that team did, it was almost like second nature for them on that defensive side. But that was the thing. His teams were so tough. But Chuck himself, he would talk to anyone, he was just such a nice guy. His team would whip an offense and then you would talk to him and you would think it couldn't be the same guy, this nice man could not be the one coaching that really tough defense.

Sam Wyche

Wyche coached the Steelers' division-rival Bengals from 1984 to 1991, during the back end of Noll's tenure in Pittsburgh. Wyche said he has always had a healthy working respect for Noll, though the duo got off to a rocky start, with Wyche seeking to show sportsmanship by shaking Noll's hand after each game and Noll keeping his hands squarely in his pockets. In the public perception, that indicated a tense relationship between the two, something Wyche said was simply not true.

CHUCK AND I were friendly. We were not friends by any stretch, but we were friendly. There was one incident, in 1985, coming off a Monday night game, we were winning and we had less than a touchdown lead at the end of the game. There were still almost two minutes left, it was not like it was the last play of the game. One of our running backs, James Brooks, had a big play, he ran in a long touchdown late in the game on fourth down. Rather than kick a field goal, we ran the ball and wound up getting the touchdown. We weren't running up the score, but there were those who thought we were.

As we come off the field, Chuck is ticked off because he lost the game, just like I am when I lose a game, and I do my thing, which is to run across and shake hands with the opposing coach. Well, he had his hands in his pockets and his head down, he was grumbling to himself. I had my hand out, the cameras were in tight on us and it was Monday Night Football, so a lot of people watching. Whoever was doing that game said on the air, 'There is a lot of bad blood between those two guys.' That was said over that one picture, but I can tell you, it was not that way at all. He just didn't want to shake hands, and I thought coaches should do that. I would try and he would try not to, he would keep his hands in his pockets. I remember the reporters asked him why I kept trying and he said, 'Maybe he wants to get some exercise.'

But he was nothing but friendly off the field. We were at a meeting of the league one year, and he approached me and Chuck said, 'Sam, you realize you are the only active coach with a winning record against me?' I said, 'No, I did not know that and I don't believe that I have that winning record.' It sure did not feel like I did. At the time, I had been fired by the Bengals and was at Tampa. I thought, all I could remember was the losses to the Steelers, not the wins. He said that I was 10-6 against the Steelers in Cincinnati though, and I was surprised to find that out. I told him, I did not know that stat but I should have a plaque made up for it. It still doesn't feel quite right, he was just such a great coach.

He is one of the best coaches in the NFL, I would put him in the upper echelon of any coach. He got the most out of his guys, that is for sure. In the days before revenue sharing, the funny thing was, we had just about the same budget in Cincinnati that the Steelers did, but our budget was always a problem and with their budget, they managed to win a lot more championships than we did. They had a pretty tight budget, I know that. But that was because of Chuck.

Marv Levy

Coach

Teams: Kansas City Chiefs, 1978-82; Buffalo Bills, 1986-97

Marv Levy was a head coach for seenteen seasons in the NFL, going 143-112 and splitting eight regular-season matchups against Noll and the Steelers during that time. He was inducted into the Hall of Fame in 2001.

THEY ARE A tremendous example of a philosophy I always had which was on display with Chuck, and that was, offense sells tickets, kicking wins games, defense wins championships. I always believed that was the way that Chuck Noll and the Steelers approached things. I had just great respect for them, they set the tone with an unbelievable defense. When I was coaching in Kansas City, you would see that defense and it would start with Joe Greene, and you would have Jack Ham and Lambert and L.C. Greenwood, all those guys. We played them in my second year in Kansas City and I just remember we could not move the ball against them.

I knew Chuck fairly well. You would always see him at the league meetings, and we competed against him so many times over the years.

I had so much respect for the way he coached his teams. There was no fluff about him, no bluster, he was a hard worker and it was a fine organization, he got along well with everyone in the organization, you never heard rumors or stories about this faction against that faction, not with the Steelers. Everyone was on the same page there, it seemed from the outside. He was an opponent and a friend.

I did not know this but I was retired, and after I retired, I bought a home in Williamsburg, Virginia, because I had coached at William and Mary in the '60s. So I bought a home there. I was at the supermarket doing some shopping and I came around the corner and my cart banged another cart coming around the corner, and I look up and it is Chuck Noll. I told him I was going to throw a flag on him. I did not even know it, but he had a house built in Williamsburg near a winery.

Rod Rust

Rod Rust first met Noll in 1967, when he was coaching at North Texas and Noll was scouting Rust's star player, Joe Greene. The two kept in touch over the years, and Rust became a well-respected assistant coach in Philadelphia, Kansas City, and New England. When Frank Gansz was fired as head coach of the Chiefs in 1988, the team fired Rust, the defensive coordinator, too. That's when Rust joined Noll in the same role in Pittsburgh.

I **WAS THE HEAD** coach at North Texas and Joe Greene was a junior, Chuck came and watched spring practice. Joe was a magnet for scouts, and Chuck watched us practice a lot. When Chuck was first named the coach of the Steelers, he had been with Shula in Baltimore, so in 1969 he got the job and he called me up and offered me a job to go work for him in Pittsburgh. I told him I would look at it, but he was not sure what my job was going to be and I was not sure about going into a situation like that. He just liked the way I coached and told me, 'We will figure out your title later.' I considered it a high compliment, but I stayed where I was.

A few years later, I was out of work and I called him and asked him if he had a job, and he said, 'I guess the shoe's on the other foot now.' He was good natured about it, but he teased me a little. Later, I was out of a job in Kansas City, we all got fired. So that time, it was the third time and the third time is the charm. He said, 'Well, you turned me down once, I turned you down once, so now let's start over at even.' He hired me in 1989 and that turned out to be a really great year. Working with Chuck Noll was one of the great pleasures of my career, really.

When I went there they did not have a computer system for scouting or anything like that. Their video guy, Mack, was a good friend to me when I was there. He had an editing system for cut-ups on video. I went and talked to him, and he and I devised a system to take what was on the video and turn them into printouts that covered what I thought I really had to know, as far as material for tendencies and that sort of thing.

He and I were going over the printouts one day, and Chuck walks in. Chuck says, 'What are you guys doing?' So we told him, we thought we had come up with something more efficient for scouting. Chuck was interested and he started asking all kinds of questions, but the technology was not really his thing. But he still kept asking, saying, 'Why don't you try this? Can we do this?' On and on and on, he dominated the conversation for an hour. Mack and I had worked out this system, and we thought it was pretty good. We were supposed to be saving time, that was the idea, but we waited a whole hour explaining and answering to Chuck and all his suggestions. So when Chuck finally left, we looked at each other, Mack said, 'Let's make an agreement. Next time we are doing this and Chuck walks in, let's both shut up.' And we just broke out laughing. We adhered to that rule.

Chuck just did not like not knowing something, especially when it came to football. He always wanted to try to understand and he would not stop asking questions until he got it. He has so much intellectual curiosity. That's a good quality.

Dick Vermeil

Over the course of nearly twenty years in NFL coaching, Dick Vermeil developed a close friendship with Noll—hardly surprising, given the amiable personalities of the two. Vermeil never coached against Noll as a conference rival, but as the coach of the Eagles from 1976 to 1982 helped lift Pennsylvania's "other" football team to the Steelers' level, reaching Super Bowl XV in 1981. Vermeil, a native of Calistoga, Calif., who coached at Napa Junior College and Stanford, bonded with Noll over their shared appreciation for that region's top export. Vermeil remained in contact with Noll until Noll's death in 2014.

CHUCK NOLL WAS a big-time Napa Valley wine enthusiast. Big-time. He knew I was from the Napa Valley, born and raised. So whenever he would see me at meetings for the league, or even for pregame warm-ups, whenever we had a moment, he would come up and ask me about what was going on with the Napa Valley wines that year, how were the Cabernets looking, all of that kind of thing. Whenever they would get the chance to play a preseason game in San Francisco or Oakland, he would go out early and tell me about it after, where he had gone and what he had tasted, what he liked. He would always collect those Napa Valley wines, and when I would see him, he would tell me the stories.

In 1979, I hired Sid Gilman with the Eagles. Sid Gilman and Chuck Noll were old friends, they had worked together a long time before that, Sid was a mentor to Chuck. Sid Gilman always told me, he was the finest teacher he had ever been around. He was the kind of guy, I felt comfortable calling him and asking him advice, he would always be willing to talk to me and share what he could—and I would listen to him, believe me. I was a young coach, and he would always give me advice. We went to the Super Bowl in 1980, and I was 44 years old going to the Super Bowl. I needed a little help, I called him and he was just so gracious, he laid out, these are the days you need to be doing this, you will give the guys off this day and maybe that day, you should watch film, he just was very clear about how to do it. What to expect, how to handle it. He had been there and he had done it, but he was not arrogant, he would gladly share information with you. He had great players of course, but he drilled those players well, he had a personal connection to those players and he got the most out of them. He had great leadership skills, too.

Because of Chuck Noll's interest in wine, we were playing a preseason game in Philadelphia against the Steelers, and I was able to put together a beautiful case of red wine, because I knew people in Napa Valley and I could get some different things that maybe Chuck didn't know about. I put that case together and took it to the visiting team locker room and put it in his locker for Chuck. We played them in the game, we handled them pretty easily, it was 36-20 in the end but it was not that close, really. We hit them pretty hard, and I think Terry Bradshaw was out of that game and Chuck was just not happy with his guys at all. So I go to midfield after the game, and Chuck comes and meets me to shake hands, and smiles at me. He says, 'Vermeil, don't ever set me up with a case of Cabernet again if this is what you're going to do to my team.'

Before he died, when Chuck was not doing well, he was already suffering from Alzheimer's and I knew he was sick. I called his wife,

Marianne, and I asked her how Chuck was doing. She said to me, I will never forget this statement, she said to me, 'The wind is at his back, Dick.' He was very ill. I asked her if he still enjoyed red wine, was that something he could still take part in. She said yes. I sent him a case of Vermeil wine. I would say that was a year before he passed away. It was just a small thing, but I just wanted to do something for him, he had done so much for me and so much for the game.

CHAPTER 14

LOCAL HEROES

In January 1992, the Steelers officially moved on from Chuck Noll by bringing in a well-respected assistant coach from the Chiefs, Bill Cowher, who did not exactly have an easy path to the job, having to beat out Dave Wannstedt and Steelers hero Joe Greene. But Cowher impressed Dan Rooney with his enthusiasm and his vision for the team. Though he was just 34 years old, Cowher had grown up five miles outside of Pittsburgh in Crafton, Pa., and his toughness and fist-pumping passion provided a nice contrast to the ever-stoic Noll. For those who worried that Cowher was too young for the job, there was this tidbit: Noll had been only thirty-seven years old when he was hired in 1969. That generally earned Cowher the benefit of the doubt.

Cowher also benefited from a fast start, winning his first three games as Steelers coach and finishing the season 11-5, earning Pittsburgh's first AFC Central crown since 1984 and its best record since the last Super Bowl team went 12-4 in 1979. Cowher won Coach of the Year honors for that. The Steelers had a first-week bye in the postseason but ran into a Buffalo Bills team that seemed to be playing with destiny on its side, having come back from a record 35-3 deficit in their playoff opener, behind backup quarterback Frank Reich.

Don Beebe

Wide Receiver

Teams: Buffalo Bills, 1989-94; Carolina Panthers, 1995; Green Bay Packers, 1996-97

Beebe played nine seasons in the NFL, six with the high-powered Bills'
offense. He averaged 82 yards per game in three regular-season games
against Pittsburgh and had a four-touchdown performance in Buffalo in
1991. He was a key player in the Bills' win over Pittsburgh in Cowher's
first playoff game, catching six passes for a team-high 72 yards.

THEY WERE A different team that year because they had the new
coach, Bill Cowher, they were playing really aggressive defense,
they definitely had some new energy. We had to go to Pittsburgh for
that and going into Steelers territory, it is just a hornets' nest, it is a
tough place to play and a tough place to get a win. Frank Reich was
the quarterback in that game, Jim Kelly was hurt during the win over
Houston, that was the big comeback game in the first playoff game.
Going into that game, when we knew Frank was quarterbacking, we
just tried to rally around him as much as we could. That team we
had, we just really excelled in the playoffs—except the Super Bowls,
obviously. But we were just a team on a roll at that point, and we had
a lot more playoff experience than they had had, we had been in the
two Super Bowls before that.

They played a lot of cover-2. Against a scheme like that, the Dick
LeBeau–style scheme, the Steelers could take out your main receiver,
or even two receivers. But we had Andre Reed and James (Lofton) and
myself and Thurman Thomas out of the backfield. That is hard to stop.
Maybe they put too much emphasis on one guy, and it left too many
other guys open. Rod is one of the greatest of all time, no one would
argue that, but he is only one guy and he could not cover all of us.

For us, you are going against one of the greats of all time in Rod
Woodson. Their defense was really good, they were a big-play defense.
You had plenty of incentive to go in there and play well. I think the
big thing was that Woodson had gotten hit and had to leave the
game, I think he was out for a while, and they brought in a backup
(nickelback Sammy Walker) and we were able to take advantage of

that. Frank was a smart quarterback, he went right after the new guy. I remember Lofton had a touchdown a nice fade pattern game against them, and we had control of the game, but I think the big thing was that our defense was very good and kept them under a lot of pressure in that game, and our running game, Thurman Thomas (54 yards) and Kenneth Davis (104 yards), they took a lot of pressure off Frank.

When you go into a place like Pittsburgh, you had better be able to jump on them early and maybe take the crowd out of it as much as possible. We were able to do that in that playoff game. But I remember being there on a Monday night one time (in November 1993) and Jim Kelly got hurt early in that game, too, and Frank came in and it was a disaster, I mean, we got smoked, it was a shutout (23-0). That was a game where you kind of said, 'OK, this team is going to be a good one for a while.' In that game, there was one play that Gary Jones, one of their safeties came in and put the hardest hit on me I ever felt, the hardest I have ever been hit. I got by D.J. Johnson and I caught a ball in the void area of the cover-2, on the outside down sideline and Jones was the safety. I caught the ball on the sideline and Gary came in and hit me so hard—he put his helmet right into my facemask, he hit me so hard, it bent my facemask right into my face. That's how hard he hit me. It was like being in a car accident. He knocked me out cold before I even hit the ground. How I caught the ball is a miracle in itself, I think my nerves just sort of took over and it was an unconscious kind of thing. I made the catch, but it was still like it was a hit that got the crowd more into it, and we were doomed.

I always thought that Jim played well against them, too. It was a little extra incentive for him because he grew up around there and was always a Steeler fan, so there was always a little extra incentive for him. That probably explains why we were able to play well, why my numbers were good—because Jim's numbers were good. For me, one of my best games ever was against the Steelers at home, in I think it was my third year in the league (in 1991, Beebe had 10 catches for 112 yards and four touchdowns against Pittsburgh in Week 2). That was when

Jim Kelly went for six touchdowns, and I don't think he ever went for six in any other game in his career. I had four of those six. Rod was on that team, and Carnell Lake was a safety, those are pretty good defensive backs, and you had D.J. Johnson on that team, too, and Thomas Everett. They could cover and they could hit hard.

But we had an advantage because of the no-huddle, that kept those guys off-balance. Three out of the four touchdowns I caught were ad-libbed at the line of scrimmage. We would get right to the line, and Jim would look at who was on the other side of me, whether it was D.J. or Rod or Carnell Lake, and he would have an idea what they were going to do and he would signal me a route. Jim would get to the line in the no-huddle and he would go, '4-4! 85! 85!' Four-four would be the formation, that's trips right, and 85 would be for the outside guys to do comeback routes. But then he would look at me and he would give each route a different number. So an 8 would be a post, or a 2 would be a slant. He would call 85, the comeback routes, and if the Steelers knew that, they would be ready for it. But then he would signal me a separate number and that is what I would run. That is what he was doing against Pittsburgh, they would line up and he would adjust on the line, flash me a different number than the play call, flash it low where they couldn't see it, and we wound up getting four touchdowns that way, three of them on plays at the line.

That was one of Jim's best games ever. I don't know what it was about the Steelers, because historically, they are such a great defense, but when we went and played them, we always had our best games.

In 1993, Rod Woodson won the NFL's Defensive Player of the Year award, intercepting eight passes and anchoring a ball-hawking defense that got the Steelers into the playoffs for the second consecutive year. Though it witnessed a career high in interceptions, 1993 might not have even been his best season—he was at least as good in 1992, and Pittsburgh's 1990 defense was the best one for which Woodson played. But picking Woodson's best season is a bit of a fool's errand. He played 10 years in Pittsburgh and made the Pro Bowl in seven of them. Most impressive, he was named to the NFL's 75th Anniversary team in 1994, as one of the four greatest defensive backs in history, alongside Mel Blount, Mike Haynes, and Dick "Night Train" Lane, when he was just eight years into his career.

In a breakup as painful as that with Terry Bradshaw or Franco Harris, salary-cap concerns, a torn-up knee suffered in 1995, and the inability to come to contract terms led Woodson to leave Pittsburgh after the 1996 season, at age 32. The necessity for the move hit Woodson hard. "I am leaving," he told the *New York Times* at the time, "and I have made this decision with my heart. Disappointed? Yes. But more than that, I am hurt. And if it hurts, then that says that this team and this city, to me, meant a lot."

Though Woodson went on to play for three other organizations—San Francisco, the Ravens, and the Raiders—he always remained a Steeler first and foremost.

Warren Moon

Playing in the AFC Central with the Oilers, Moon saw Woodson twice a year and does not have the fond memories of Cowher's first season in NFL that some in Pittsburgh do. That's because Moon was KO'd by Woodson in Week 8 in Pittsburgh, a game the Oilers wound up losing, 21-20, when they gave up 14 unanswered points to the Steelers in the fourth quarter.

TO ME, ROD Woodson was one of the best three or four corners to play the game. He gave me my last concussion, in 1992.

It was a strong safety blitz, and he knocked me to the turf, he hit me right up near my chin and I went down. My head hit up against that Three Rivers turf and that stuff was like concrete. It was the worst in the league. That was my last concussion in the NFL. I went down and I did not remember anything for something like a 20-minute span. I still don't. We were winning that game, but I got knocked out, they wound up making a comeback and won that game. But Rod was great because he was not just a cover-guy, he was a great hitter and a great tackler that way. He was so versatile, I never knew where they were going to have him lined up. He could be on the corner one play, he could be at the nickel the next play, he could be at safety. He always made big plays, and then they'd line him up at returner and he could hurt you that way. He was one of the best players I ever played against, at any position.

Bobby Hebert

Quarterback

Team: New Orleans Saints, 1985–92; Atlanta Falcons, 1993–96

The 1993 Steelers were inconsistent on their way to a 9-7 record, but they did have a four-game stretch in the early part of the season in which they went 4-0 and outscored opponents 132-41. Woodson was a key to that stretch, especially in a 45-17 throttling of the Falcons in Atlanta. Hebert was the starting quarterback in that game but was replaced by Billy Joe Tolliver, who threw two interceptions to Woodson.

THAT GAME WAS just one where they got the ball rolling and I tell you what, they just snowballed us. I think it was a Monday night game. What a nightmare. They kept coming and coming. I got pulled from that game and they put in Billy Joe and lucky for me, Woodson got the two interceptions on him. But that is what I always remember if you are a quarterback playing them. I would go up to the line and look around and say, 'OK, where's Woodson?' And even if you saw him, he was a smart cornerback, he was going to be able to do something where he might line up in one spot and make you think he was going to drop into a certain coverage, but he was just trying to bait you all along to throw it where he wanted you to throw it. He could do everything, he could come on the blitz, he could just shut down your main guy, he could help. He was a heck of a kick returner too, early on in his career. He could have played on the offensive side if that is what he wanted to do.

Rod Rust

In Rust's one season in Pittsburgh, he altered the coverage scheme of the team's defensive backs and showed Woodson different ways to think and prepare in order to get the most out of his physical gifts. Rust saw that as simply doing his job as a coach, but when Woodson was inducted into the Hall of Fame in 2009, Rust got a surprise when he listened to Woodson's speech.

HE WAS SUCH a phenomenal athlete, and that was common knowledge, that he was the best athlete in the league, it didn't take long to figure that out. I had a conversation with him, late spring or early summer, before that 1989 season, and he later said it struck a nerve with him. I told him, 'You're going to have a great career because you have such innate talent. It'll go on until age steals your explosiveness. But now the question is, during the early part of your career here, can you study the game? Can you become accomplished at the mental part of it? Because if you do, when your explosiveness goes away, you will be smart enough to play another six or seven years.'

He never talked to me about it after that. But when he was inducted into the Hall of Fame, I am sitting there watching his Hall of Fame speech, and to this day, one of the most satisfying moments of my coaching career was when he was talking, he said his usual thank-yous, and he mentioned Chuck. Then he mentioned me. I was only there one year. But what he said was, he thanked me for challenging him. And I was very humbled by that. I was not even challenging him, really, I was just projecting and telling him from what I had seen, what he would be able to do in this sport. He took it as a challenge to learn the mental part of the game though, and he sure did that. I told him one time, early, at the start of the 4-deep technique, I told him, 'If you can see the stem of the second receiver, you're about 75 percent sure what the wide receiver is going to run.' He had not heard that before, but once I told him, it was like he got the keys to the bank. He started understanding a lot more—but that was all from him. He saw that things got easier for him the more he studied. There was nothing special about the information I was passing to him, it was just that he took it and really tried to learn from it and wanted to learn more and more.

That secondary was really special. Rod Woodson was young, and we had Carnell Lake, and Carnell was a tremendous athlete but he was a rookie. Something that a lot of people don't know, wouldn't know, was that Larry Griffin was such an important part of that team because he had been the starter. We installed Carnell as the starter coming out of training camp because he was just so fast, he was a really great athlete and Larry Griffin was a journeyman athlete. But he had been around and he was disciplined, smart enough to not make mistakes. We were a better defense with Larry because Carnell did the things rookies do. But Larry stayed with us and he helped Carnell just about every day he was there, he was working with him and helping him learn the game. Carnell had just taken his job. But

Larry was a total professional and just wanted to help this young guy get better. The guy who was as good as any of them was Thomas Everett. For a little guy, he was such a great hitter. He was only 5-9 but he could hit. I don't like saying this, because I don't like seeing guys get hurt—and Thomas did not like that either—but he was the guy who ended Al Toon's career. First play of the game, they threw it to Al Toon over the middle, and Thomas came flying out of the middle and laid Al Toon out. It wasn't a dirty hit, it was just Thomas Everett playing football. It is still a sad day to me, when that happened. That was what Thomas could do, that group was like that. But it was obvious that Rod was a special, special player on that unit.

CHAPTER 15

RESILIENCE

In 1994, the Steelers appeared to be a team that had finally put its pieces together. After a 5-3 start, Pittsburgh won seven straight games and, along the way, developed a brashness anchored by its defense, which ranked second in the NFL in points and yardage allowed. Linebackers Kevin Greene and Greg Lloyd combined for 24 sacks on the season, and each—along with Rod Woodson—earned a Pro Bowl berth. The running back trio of Barry Foster (who missed six weeks with a knee injury), rookie Bam Morris, and fullback John L. Williams combined for more than 2,000 yards rushing; and Neil O'Donnell was a steady, if unexciting, presence at quarterback.

The Steelers earned a spot in the AFC Championship game, and were 9.5-point favorites over the Chargers, but suffered an upset loss at Three Rivers Stadium.

Bobby Ross

Coach

Teams: San Diego Chargers, 1992-96; Detroit Lions, 1997-2000

Bobby Ross had been an assistant with Kansas City during the Steel Curtain years in the late 1970s but had spent the bulk of his head-coaching career at the collegiate level, coaching at Maryland from 1982 to 1986 and Georgia Tech from 1987 to 1991. He made the leap to the ranks of NFL head coaches the same year as Bill Cowher, 1992, taking over the Chargers and, like Cowher, bringing an immediate turnaround, finishing 11-5 after San Diego had gone 4-12 the previous year. In 1994, the Chargers went 11-5, beating the Steelers in the season finale in a game in which Cowher rested many of his starters.

THE THING THAT I remember, I always had great respect for the Steelers program. The Rooney family, they're wonderful people. Bill Cowher, I had a lot of respect for, he did a tremendous job coaching and I don't think anyone would handle the pressure of the job the way he did, taking over for a guy like Chuck Noll and still going out and making it your own team. But he did that, they played very much like him, by that I mean, they took on his personality and his intensity and love for the game. Their quarterback, Neil O'Donnell, was a young man I had recruited for the University of Maryland, so I knew him quite well. But they were a team you always respected because of what they did physically on the field, they were perhaps the most physical team in the National Football League in my time.

Going into that game, we were heavy underdogs and we knew that. We had played them in the regular season, and it was the last game of the season, on Christmas. We won that game but Bill had pulled his starters early. We were playing for a home field advantage, so in that respect, we had more at stake. So we won the game, it was a tight game, it was 37-34, and we were fortunate to get that win. But Pittsburgh had nothing at stake in that game, so they got what they wanted out of the game, and we finally got what we wanted, too, the victory. We won our first playoff game at home against Miami, and that was a tough one, too, because we had to come back to win that game and Miami missed a field goal at the end that would have won it.

We went to Pittsburgh for the AFC Championship game, we got there and we had heard that the players, the Steelers players, had already reserved a banquet room for a celebration. I still don't know if that was true or not true. But our players had heard it, and they were offended by it, that they were not getting much respect from Pittsburgh. Junior Seau, our linebacker, said to me, we had a night meeting like everybody does before the game, and Junior came to me and said, 'Coach, we have heard some things about this banquet, do you mind if I talk to the team?' I said, 'Not at all. Take your time, have as much time as you want.' Junior could be very emotional, as I think most people know. So he started talking, and he got into an emotional talk to our squad. It was not a tirade or anything like that, it was just very emotional. He talked about respect, he talked about earning respect.

We got to the game, and as was always the case, Pittsburgh was playing very physical, and we were struggling. Our defense was keeping us in the game, but our offense just could not do a whole lot with the ball, offensively speaking. Defensively, we had Bill Arnsparger as our defensive coordinator, and Bill was a bend-but-don't-break type of a guy. That was what we were doing. We were bending a lot, they were moving between the 20s, but we were not breaking. A decisive play in the game, which I think just because of our great respect for them and their physical play was such a big, big play for us because it was a physical play we happened to win. It was the thing that ignited us. We ran a toss sweep with Natrone Means, and Natrone was a physical runner. He was about, I guess, 240, 245 and had some athletic skills as well, was a very good receiver, too. We were battling and just looking for a breakthrough play. They had a great safety at the time, Carnell Lake, who was known for his hitting, he was a great hitter. Lake came up and he smacked Natrone, but Natrone won the battle. He didn't evade him. He ran over him, and Lake just went down, Natrone kept running. That was a very unusual thing for us. That ignited our sideline, our whole team came up off the bench. For the first time, they saw us do something physical that was perhaps equal to them at the time.

I thought that was a turning point for us because it gave us a tremendous confidence lift. We were down by a touchdown at that point, but that helped us realize, 'Hey we have got some physical play to us as well.' You have to play that way against Pittsburgh if you are going to have any kind of a chance. I thought that was a key, key play for us. We never, throughout the ball game, moved the ball all that great, but we had big plays. We had a big play, a long throw to Al Pupunu from Stan that gave us a touchdown, and we had a long throw to Tony Martin that gave us a touchdown off a play action, we fooled them on that. We had a penalty, a pass interference penalty that gave us field position and we got a field goal out of that. But we needed big plays to win that game. We didn't do a whole lot else offensively otherwise.

The big thing was the final drive, the final two minutes. They got the ball and it was 17-13, they needed a touchdown. We were bending and not breaking, but Neil was playing very well, he was making smart passes and he was driving them down. I got very uncomfortable, I went to Bill, he called the defenses, and I said, 'What have we got to stop this thing?' And he said, 'We'll keep trying to play it, and I will mix a little more pressure into it.' We got down to the last play. Fourth down, I think it was the 3-yard line. They went with a dropback pass and Neil went to the running back, (Barry) Foster, and our linebacker Dennis Gibson came up. We had gotten him from Detroit, we had lost a very good linebacker in Gary Plummer when he signed with the 49ers, and Gibson was his replacement. Gibson came up and made a great play and we got the win. But they were three yards from the Super Bowl.

Mark Brunell

Quarterback

Teams: Green Bay Packers, 1994; Jacksonville Jaquars, 1995-2003; Washington Redskins, 2004-06; New Orleans Saints, 2008-09; New York Jets, 2010-11

Mark Brunell spent his rookie season in Green Bay but went to Jacksonville in 1995, the Jaguars' expansion season. There, in Week 6, he faced Pittsburgh in a home game and managed the Jaguars' first win in Jacksonville, throwing for 189 yards and a touchdown in a 20-16 win. But the Steelers' front seven made Brunell pay, racking up four sacks.

TO ME, IT always started with their level of talent because they were always solid up front, their linebackers and the line. They always had a certain type of player, sort of ideal football players—tough, physical, smart. You knew you were always going to play guys who were good guys at their positions. That, combined with their schemes, the zone blitzes, the constant pressure, the multiple disguises. That was the one team that always gave me fits as far as preparing for them and playing against them.

Carnell Lake stands out to me on the corner. Levon Kirkland, he was probably the biggest 'Mike' backer I ever faced in my career. Greg Lloyd, Kevin Greene, all the guys from that era were just such good football players. Lloyd was just fierce. The thing about him was that he did not say much, he just got up and played hard. He was really physical, aggressive, and smart. He was really good at what he did. The pressure schemes, their ability to disguise. They were always bringing pressure, and they were not going to give away anything. They were hard to read, you always had to be on your toes. Your presnap reads, the looks they were giving you, you had to constantly be checking because chances are, what they were showing you before the snap was not what they were doing after the snap. It was particularly difficult as a young guy going against these guys because you have not seen a lot of those things until you have gone through the league a few times. You had your work cut out for you.

We got our first home win for the Jaguars, 1995 against Pittsburgh. Not an easy thing to do, and that win really lifted our whole season, you measured yourself against those guys. When you play the

Steelers, you could count on four or five sacks, that was just going to happen. And it was not always the line's fault, sometimes it was the quarterback not making the right read and checking out of the play. But that was something I learned playing against them, that you were going to get hit but you just kind of get back to the line and not let it affect you, just try to make the read the next time. They disguise very well—multiple fronts, multiple coverages. That 3-4 presents problems, more than a 4-3 typically does. It is a tough system, but what makes it tough is the players they had. You can't just plug anybody into a Dick LeBeau system and they'll be good, that's crazy. They were very good at identifying who could play in that system and letting them succeed in that.

If you ask former Packers safety LeRoy Butler about the Pittsburgh Steelers, he knows exactly what you want to talk about. "Don't tell me," Butler says. "The Yancey Thigpen game." Indeed, after the heartbreak of the 1994 AFC Championship, the 1995 season looked like it might be a disaster in the early part of the year, with Rod Woodson's knee injury and a 3-4 start. But the Steelers won seven straight games, and wide receiver Yancey Thigpen set new Pittsburgh records for catches (85) and yards (1,307). They just needed to get to 12 wins to secure the AFC's top overall seed. The Packers, meanwhile, had been in a 23-year doldrums, a historically proud franchise that had not won a division title since 1972. When they met the Steelers in Green Bay in the last game of the 1995 season, the Packers needed a win in order to break that string and take the NFC Central.

They got a miracle. With the Packers up, 24-19, and a light snow falling at Lambeau Field, the Steelers mounted a clock-chewing final drive that used up more than five minutes and brought them all the way to the Green Bay 6-yard line. On a fourth-down play, Neil O'Donnell found Thigpen wide open in the left corner after Thigpen managed to turn cornerback Craig Newsome around, but when the ball got to Thigpen's waiting hands, it just kept zipping right through. Thigpen could not squeeze the pass, and the Packer faithful erupted in cheers. The Packers would advance to the conference championship, where they felt they had a good matchup against the Cowboys and a potential rematch with Pittsburgh. Alas, Dallas won the NFC and wound up facing the Steelers in that year's Super Bowl.

Leroy Butler

Defensive Back

Team: *Green Bay Packers, 1990-2001*

Butler was a four-time Pro Bowl safety, playing all 12 seasons of his career in Green Bay. He had 38 career interceptions but remains best known as the originator of the "Lambeau Leap," the post-touchdown celebration in which Packers players jump into the first row of fans. And, being a Packer legend and all, he didn't necessarily want to cop to this, but it is true: he grew up a huge Cowboys fan and developed a deep loathing for the Steelers when he was a kid in the late '70s.

IJUST REMEMBER FOR us, the playoffs were a big deal at that time, we were trying to get Green Bay back to where the Packers are supposed to be. To beat the Steelers with the chance to go to the playoffs was a feat most teams, I don't think, would be able to pull off. Especially when you look at the personnel that Steelers team had, they went to the Super Bowl that year. We had gone through a coaching change and we were getting ourselves together. But beating the Steelers at Lambeau Field, in the snow, what could be better than that? It was a lot of pressure on us, I don't think people know the pressure we had on us in that game. People in Green Bay knew, but I don't think, nationally, people knew. We had everything on that.

They had that great running game, Morris the big guy and the fast guy, Pegram. They had Kordell Stewart, too, he was someone we felt like we needed to know where he was at all times. Kordell, I will tell you what now, he won't ever get the credit he deserves, but we used to call him the Swiss Army knife. Whatever you need. Quarterback, wide receiver, running back, he could do it all. Corkscrew, scissors. He was the Swiss Army knife. They were not using him as a quarterback much at that point, but they would run him and line him up as a wideout. He had that Slash thing, it was all in everybody's head—are they going to have him go over the middle and get matched up on the linebacker? Are they going to get him going to the outside? You had to have a defense ready for him, almost like a box-and-one in basketball. He just added a dimension that teams don't use anymore, but man, he was valuable. They had him, and that power running game, it was a match made in heaven. He was dynamic. He could run away from linebackers if you put them on him, he was as fast as DBs, and he could throw it like any other quarterback. He was a weapon.

It was probably the most intense game-planning of any game I had been in, you know, not including the playoffs. They had a lot of bad matchups for us one-on-one so we played a lot of combination zones and things of that nature. We knew they were going to be a well-coached team because of Bill Cowher, the Steelers always were well coached, we just knew we had to execute. That's what Coach Mike (Holmgren) was saying, we gotta execute. A team like the Steelers, they can embarrass you if you don't execute.

Bam Morris was one of those guys, we watched film and we were joking about it, he was just so big, he was like tackling a bowling ball. Bam Morris if he catches it in the flat area and you go up to make the tackle, he is going to put his foot in your chest and run right over you. We even had a thing on our board, we drew him on our dry erase board and the question that was up there was, 'How can you tackle a guy this size?' But it was a serious question. We looked at films on teams that dealt with him, tackled him before he got started, that was the best way to deal with him because once he got going, it was not easy. We looked at teams that did not have success against him, teams that let him get to the secondary, and we were watching film of all the dead bodies he had run over. It was a good mixture with him and Pegram, two different guys and how do you defend that? So we would have two packages, we would be run-heavy when Morris was in the game and then be able to dial it back when you felt like they were going to throw it.

But that last drive was tense. We practiced that kind of thing in practice every Friday, situational football. If we have a lead, if the game is close, if they have a lead, how much time is left. They used to run a lot of these rub routes. They would not call them pick plays because you could not do those, but they would call them rub routes, where it just sort of looks like you are going to hit someone and you have to kind of rub off them. We knew it was a possibility that we were going to have a matchup problem somewhere. Thigpen had such a great year, he was catching everything and he ran really good, solid routes.

They were driving, and we just were so concerned with making sure we had a matchup somewhere, that every one of us was matched up with a receiver. We were calling out, every play, 'Match up! Match up!' We knew it was going to come down to one or two plays. They were conducting themselves, really, like a team that knew they were going to score. Like it was no big deal. You have to tip your cap to a team that has that level of confidence. They got down there, inside our 10 and they drew up the perfect play for Thigpen against the defense we had, and he was wide open. It was a perfect play. It was almost as if they knew what defense we were in. I turned and saw where he was, saw he was open and thought that was it. But then I heard the roar of the crowd and I knew he had dropped it. But in his defense, the weather was not all that great. It was snowing, it was muddy. So maybe there were some factors. But I saw that, I knew we won, and I jumped up in the stands.

Remember, the Steelers were a team we all grew up watching. Now, I will be honest, I had a little vendetta against the Steelers. This goes back deep, this goes maybe more than people want to know. But this is breaking news: I was a huge Cowboys fan. I was the bigger Cowboys fan than the people in the Cowboys organization. I was a huge Roger Staubach fan, I was a huge Tony Dorsett fan. I was a huge fan of that team. When Jackie Smith dropped that pass in the end zone, right? I went into my mom's room crying and upset. Literally. You don't understand. Crying. Tears coming down my face. I was saying, 'We can never beat these guys, I hate the Steelers. Why did he drop that pass?'

You have to understand, I was so upset my mom kept me out of school, I was so distraught. She was explaining to me, that's just sports, these things happen, you are not going to win every time. We just couldn't beat them. I was a kid, I grew up hating Terry Bradshaw, hating Lynn Swann, that whole tradition, the Steel Curtain. Bus (Bettis) is one of my best friends in the world and he is one of the few who knows this story, but I was just so upset and that was in the back of my mind in 1995. I will be honest. I wanted to step up and beat them. I cried too much over the Steelers when I was a kid, I felt like I deserved payback. So when Thigpen dropped that pass, I said to the football gods, 'Thank you. Now, myself as a kid, I can move on. I can move on as a Cowboys fan. I can say we are even now.' To players, maybe not to the media or even fans, but to players, that Steelers organization, their tradition, that is a team you want to beat. You want that notch on your belt. They were the best franchise. Best ownership, Chuck Noll was a god. You know those things. But I despised the black and gold.

That was a game that, I think, catapulted us to the limelight. The Steelers went to the Super Bowl that year. That was the first game that we started thinking we were building something and of course, we won the Super Bowl the next year.

Erric Pegram

Running Back

Teams: Atlanta Falcons, 1991-94; Pittsburgh Steelers, 1995-96; New York Giants and San Diego Chargers, 1997

Running back Erric Pegram remembers watching the Steelers' AFC championship matchup against the Chargers following the 1994 season and thinking he knew just what the Steelers were lacking in that game: him. Pegram was a free agent following the 1994 season and knew that with a bruising big guy like Bam Morris on hand, he could be the perfect speed back to bolster Pittsburgh's running attack. He just had to wait as the Steelers sought a taker for oft-injured bruising back Barry Foster, who was eventually dealt to Carolina.

Pegram fielded offers from several teams, but he was not shy about letting others know he wanted most to go to the Steelers and would take less money to do so. Just two years earlier, Pegram had been playing for Jerry Glanville's Falcons when the Steelers knocked them in Atlanta, 45-17. That game certainly piqued Pegram's interest in the Steelers.

I REMEMBER PLAYING AGAINST the Steelers in 1993 on a Monday night, I have to admit that I didn't know anything about the Pittsburgh Steelers football team before that Monday night matchup. During the week of preparation, I didn't recognize names like Rod Woodson, Barry Foster, Kevin Greene, or Greg Lloyd, I didn't even know who the head coach was at the time. But what I do remember about that specific game was taking a serious beating by their Blitzburgh defense, they were so dominant that I thought for sure there were 12 or 13 guys on the field. I was so convinced I actually asked the referees to count how many men were on the field. I wasn't able to run the ball effectively because of their seven- and eight-man fronts, their run-stop defense was the best I'd ever played against. So, it was two years later, of course I wanted them on my side.

FACING THE PITTSBURGH STEELERS

The Packers were one of the teams I talked to, but I told the running back coach from Green Bay, whom I don't remember, that I would take less money to sign with the Pittsburgh Steelers and I remember the running back coach asking me why. I told him if I sign with the Pittsburgh Steelers, we would go to the Super Bowl. I really believed it. And we did. It really was a common-sense decision, I watched the Steelers lose the AFC Championship in 1994 against the Chargers, a game they should have won, and I distinctly remember thinking I would love to play with the Steelers, I actually felt I was the missing piece of the puzzle. You have to excuse my brash thinking then, but pro football players, whether we admit it or not, are all a little cocky.

I signed my contract with the Steelers in 1995 in secrecy because they were trying to trade Barry Foster. They put the contract in a safe not to be made public until they dealt Barry Foster away, and for a while there, if word had gotten out that I was under contract before the Barry Foster transaction was made, the contract would be voided. They decided to sign me for the 1995 roster after Bill Cowher had a conversation with Jerry Glanville where he told Coach Cowher, it was a very stupid decision if he didn't sign me. The rest is history.

Once his contract was finally signed in Pittsburgh, Pegram had an eventful 1995 season, starting with the noticeable difference in the way the Steelers were run when compared to the Falcons, for whom Pegram played the first four years of his career. On the field, Pegram led the team with 813 yards rushing, and caught 26 passes for 206 yards out of the backfield, helping the Steelers to 407 points, the second-highest total in franchise history (416 points in 1979 were the most). He had three touchdowns in a big overtime win in Chicago and registered 110-yard days in wins over the Browns and Raiders. The Steelers trounced the Bills in the opening round of the playoffs, 40-21, and then prepared to play the Colts in Pittsburgh for a chance, for the first time since the 1979 season, to return to the Super Bowl, where the Steelers would eventually lose to the Cowboys, thanks in large part to three poor throws from O'Donnell that resulted in interceptions, two of which went to Super Bowl MVP Larry Brown.

But for Pegram, what wound up being a 20-16 win over the Colts in the AFC championship game took on a little extra meaning with a special halftime delivery. (Literally.)

Erric Pegram

I DIDN'T LEARN TO play professional football until I signed with the Steelers. My previous four years with the Falcons, that was just a start. From the time I walked into Three Rivers Stadium, I knew it was different, from the front office to the equipment manager. It felt like it was different. People ask me what was my best year in the NFL, I always say 1995 not because of my personal achievements but it's the first time on a team where the chemistry with my teammates and our goals as a team were completely in sync.

As always, it started with the head coach, Bill Cowher, a true leader of men, if he asked me today, I'd suit up and try to take the field for him, and I would not even ask any questions. On the offensive side of the ball, players like Dermontti Dawson, Justin Strzelczyk (rest in peace), Leon Searcy, Charles Johnson, Yancey Thigpen, Kordell Stewart, Bam Morris, and my wingman John L. Williams, our fullback. On the defensive side, players like Darren Perry, the run-stopper Levon Kirkland, Greg Lloyd, who is the meanest dude I've ever played with, and 'Big Play' Ray Seals. Those were just a few guys who made you want to spill your guts on Sunday for them. I remember every one of their faces, their smiles, the heartache when we lost but most importantly, I remember our struggle, the physical pain and achieving our goals as a team. That's what makes it worth it, they made you love the game for each other and I love them for that.

When we went up against the Colts, when I think about it now, there were seven plays that were significant in us winning that game. The first one was Kordell Stewart's touchdown catch at the back of the end zone, which we needed so badly because we were struggling on offense. We scored only three points in the first half, but we got that play in right before the half, and that gave us a lead, 10-6. The second play was the tipped pass by Chris Oldham right before the first half ended. Harbaugh threw a pass, and it would have been a touchdown had Chris not gotten his fingertips on that ball. The third one was the special teams play by Fred McAfee on the kick-off in the second half. He made a great hit and he was fired up, which helped set the tone for us. Fourth is the shoestring tackle by Willie Williams on Lamont Warren. They had third-and-1 and the defense made a mistake, there was a big hole for Warren. They were around the 30-yard line, but he would have scored. Instead, Willie made it over to where the play was going and just brought Warren down—if he doesn't make that tackle, we don't go to the Super Bowl, that's a fact. The fifth one was the big Ernie Mills catch from Neil O'Donnell that put us on their 1-yard line right after the two-minute warning in the fourth quarter. Like I said, we had trouble moving the ball, we were down, 16-13, and we needed a big play. They had been taking away the passing game, but that one gave us a chance to win the game. Number 6 is the touchdown that put us ahead, Bam Morris plowing through for the go-ahead touchdown after Ernie's catch.

And then there was the Hail Mary pass from Jim Harbaugh to Aaron Bailey, five seconds left, we could not see what happened, but it seemed like it took forever to be called incomplete. I literally thought I was going to have a heart attack right there on the field. The rest is a complete blur.

But, personally for me, my daughter Taylor decided to break my wife's water at 3 a.m. the morning of the game so I really didn't get a lot of sleep. I was with my wife at the hospital until about 9 a.m., and the game was at 12:30 p.m. Finally my wife told me to go, and told me to win. I was in the locker room at halftime and coming out, somebody told me I had just had a daughter, then they announced it on the scoreboard. She was born at halftime of that Colts game, so we call her Halftime Taylor. My father gave her that nickname.

I was mentally and physically ready to go. My wife just gave birth so I thought, 'All I need to do is go win a football game.' And we did.

In the wake of the Steelers' loss to the Cowboys in Super Bowl XXX, Pegram's backfield partner—Bam Morris—created a headache for Pittsburgh brass when he was arrested on drug-possession charges in Texas, a month before the NFL's draft. But uncertainty around Morris pushed the Steelers to upgrade their running game, and at the draft, they pulled off a blockbuster trade, acquiring disgruntled Rams running back Jerome Bettis along with a third-round pick for a second-round pick, plus a fourth-rounder in 1997. At the time, it was a slight gamble for the Steelers, because Bettis had feuded with coach Rich Brooks in St. Louis and his rushing total had dropped from 1,429 yards as a rookie to 637 in year 3. But by the end of Bettis's first year in Pittsburgh, the Steelers were celebrating the transaction as Bettis racked up 1,431 yards and 11 touchdowns.

Marcellus Wiley

Defensive Lineman

Teams: Buffalo Bills, 1997-2000; San Diego Chargers, 2001-03; Dallas Cowboys, 2004; Jacksonville Jaguars, 2005-06

FACING THE PITTSBURGH STEELERS

Marcellus Wiley was a Pro Bowl defensive end who came into the league with Buffalo the year after Bettis went to Pittsburgh. Eventually, the two became good friends, but on the field the Bus was a problem Wiley struggled to solve.

WE WERE PLAYING him out there at Heinz Field and this was around the time that people were starting to whisper that it was coming to an end. As difficult as it is as an athlete to go out there and play someone when they're at their best, because you have to be at your best as well, it's also a challenge when you have to play against a guy that you're hearing is not at his best but you still have to respect his greatness. And that's what Jerome Bettis was at that moment. All I remember is one play in particular, where it was a typical dive play, it was probably a 34 dive, and that play, I was shedding the offensive tackle to the inside and the tackle was still driving on me, so I guess I had one arm free and one arm still on the tackle. Not perfect technique. So obviously, I am compromised and here comes the Bus into the B gap, and I have one arm out there, my shoulder and a little bit of my head into the gap. All I remember is, when he hit my arm, which was extended out sideways, he hit it with his ass right under his feet. He hit it so hard my arm turned all the way around my back. And I am not that flexible. It was like smacking my own shoulder pad on the back. I just remember being on the ground, one of my arms is behind me almost in a surrender position and I am looking and all I see is these big, bull-looking thighs churning away and all this dirt being kicked on me. As close as you can get to the Running of the Bulls, that was it for me right here. He still was a monster. Even toward his retirement, people were saying, 'Hey, come on back.' But you know, he left right on time. With a championship.

When you have a guy like that who is built like that, there is always a moment of truth that exists that doesn't exist with a smaller guy. There's a moment of truth that, it's not about whether you can catch him, it's about what are you going to do once you get there?

That's the big difference with Jerome. A lot of times you are in such a compromised position that you can't do anything else. The scatter-bugs, you gotta run around and catch them, and as soon as you catch them, they're done. But a guy like Bettis, that's just half the battle. That's the most difficult thing about facing a guy like him, not only getting there, but once you do get there, you have got to get your wrestling on just to get him down.

To his core, one of the coolest, nicest men I've ever met, players I've ever met. And I don't throw that around easily because I've been blessed to meet many a guy, and they run the entire gamut. When you talk about the Bus, that's first class, always been the case since Day One no matter what your status is. He was a great player, and just as great a guy.

SECTION 6

DYNASTY RELOADED

CHAPTER 16

BIG BEN

I N THE EARLY fall of 2001, the sporting public in Pittsburgh was focused on the opening of the Steelers' new home, and with good reason. Gone was Three Rivers Stadium, with its cookie-cutter layout and concrete-hard turf, replaced by the glittering new Heinz Field, a stadium designed to highlight the setting on the city's North Shore with spectacular views of the Ohio River, while bringing the Steelers into the 21st century and simultaneously honoring their rich history with an open-air team museum. The Steelers played their first game on October 7. No one could know it at the time, but six days after that and 300 miles to the west, the future of the Steelers and, ultimately, their ticket to a return to championship glory were taking shape. In front of a sparse crowd at Yager Stadium in Oxford, Ohio, the Miami (Ohio) Red Hawks had taken an 18-point lead early in their game against Akron, only to witness NFL prospect Charlie Frye lead a Zips charge back to the lead, scoring a go-ahead field goal in the final moment.

But then, a miracle, one that pushed Miami freshman quarterback Ben Roethlisberger from mid-major anonymity to the national stage. Taking the ball at his own 16-yard line with seven seconds to play, Roethlisberger first fired a 14-yard out pattern to the sideline to move the Red Hawks to the 30. Then, with three seconds to play, Roethlisberger dropped back and hurled a bomb that went nearly 70 yards in the air toward the end zone. A defensive back for Akron tipped the ball, and receiver Eddie Tillitz grabbed it, stepping into the end zone for the win. The legend of Big Ben—unknown to those in Pittsburgh at the time, he was the future of the Steelers—had its first chapter.

Lee Owens

Coach

Teams: *University of Akron, 1995-2003; Ashland University, 2003-*
Lee Owens has been in the coaching business for forty years and count-
ing, and spent nine seasons at Akron. He thought he'd secured a big win
over Miami in that game in 2001 before Roethlisberger struck.

I THINK THAT GAME helped put him on the map, but the funny thing is, he never thanked me for it.

It may be the toughest loss of my coaching career, and I have had a bunch of them, so that's saying something. The crazy thing about it, I will never forget it, was that I walked by the meeting our defensive coordinator, Bob Morris, was having with the defensive backs. The last thing he did with our DBs was to cover that last play, how to cover the Hail Mary. He was talking about it to them the day before the game. And I thought, 'Wow, I can't believe he is actually covering that at the meeting.' He was going over where our guys should line up, how we are going to defend it, never tip the ball up, always bat it down. The team broke and left the meeting, and it would have to happen that it was the last thing on my mind before we got ready for that game.

It was tough. We were trying at Akron to find ways to win and be relevant, and beating a team like Miami with Roethlisberger would have been really good for us. Our quarterback was Charlie Frye, who went on to have a pretty good career of his own, in Cleveland and with Oakland. Charlie knew how big that win would be. He came over to me after we went up, when we were kicking off and said, 'Coach, this one's for you.' And I have been around long enough to know what can happen before that clock says zero, so I said, 'No, no, let's finish this thing and get this win.'

We kicked the ball to them deep, and they took a knee right away, which was smart, only a few seconds came off the clock. They had to go almost 90 yards in two plays with no timeouts. He throws a 15-yard out to the sideline and stops the clock. Now they have to go 55 yards, and with the drop-back, they have to go 70 yards on the last play with four seconds left on the clock. He goes back there, moves around, a couple guys miss him, and he just heaves it into the air. I still remember our safety there, if he had let the ball go, it would have fallen, his receiver was not going to get there. It would have been game over, we would have won. But our guy tips it in the air, and their receiver catches it in stride on the 5-yard line or so, and walks into the end zone.

I literally fell. I was not even aware of what was happening, I just fell to my knees, into the ground, hands on the ground. I was motionless. Absolutely exhausted, absolutely empty, absolutely just drained. It is the hard part of the game. I am not sure the wound has completely healed yet and it has been more than a decade. Those two plays, it was incredible. I think I tried to look up and find him and shake Ben's hand after that, but honestly, I was so stunned I am not sure if I did. It was a long bus ride home.

The good news is I have seen him do that to some pretty good teams since then in the NFL. I have seen him keep plays alive against some pretty good defenses, I have seen good players bounce off of him, and as long as he has a chance to put it up there, he is never out of it. That makes me feel a little better, I guess. Just a little.

Shane Montgomery
Offensive Coordinator

Team: *Miami University of Ohio*

Shane Montgomery was the offensive coordinator for the late head coach Terry Hoeppner, arriving at Miami for Roethlisberger's freshman year.

FACING THE PITTSBURGH STEELERS

From the beginning, it was clear that Ben had a future in football, and though the Hail Mary was his breakthrough moment as a freshman, he improved steadily as a sophomore and junior before heading into the NFL draft.

IT WAS ONE of those games where we dominated the first half and probably should have been up more. Then the second half comes, and you're frustrated because you can't get anything going, and they came back and kicked the field goal to put them up by three with maybe nine seconds left. On the sideline, you're just demoralized, and I was up in the box at the time and we decided to take a knee off the squib kick and try to save some time and see if we could set things up. We threw an out, like a 14-yard out and got out of bounds with about four seconds left. At that point, it is a Hail Mary—we actually called it Big Ben. We practiced it, we practiced it every week. But it is the kind of thing you probably could go four years without ever needing it. What was really important was the way he was able to move around, because that gave us time to get down there in position. He threw it up, maybe 65 or 70 yards in the air. It deflected off one of their guys and our receiver got it and ran it in. For him to be able to get it even close to the end zone from that spot, it was pretty amazing. He had already done some good things for us before that, but that was kind of when he started to really take off, his name really got out there, being able to make that play to win a game.

When I first saw him that first spring, I thought he could be pretty good. He was a lot thinner than what you think of now, of course, maybe 200 pounds. But he had a strong arm. That first year, like any young quarterback, he was not where he needed to be physically, and it wears on you. The first two games we played his first year were at Michigan and at Iowa, those were his first two career games. He had only played one year at quarterback in high school. One of the first plays of his career, we were playing in Michigan, and he got his nose broken. He didn't miss playing time because of it, but I think it made the light go on for him, that he was going to have to really change his body in order to keep up with these guys who were so much bigger and faster. You saw him start taking that more seriously after that. He knew he had to be able to take a hit.

The one thing he has always had is great pocket presence, even as a youngster. He can escape rushes, he can move around in the pocket and avoid those big hits, he has always been able to do that. He wasn't a guy who was necessarily going to run for big chunks of yards, but he was able to move in the pocket and avoid taking the big hits, and that really saves his body a lot. In the three years we had him, he did not miss any games, and I am not sure he even missed any plays. He was just able to be smart enough to read what was going on, and he has a lot of confidence in his ability, and that helps, too. The mobility in the pocket, that takes a lot of wear and tear off of him.

We played in the shotgun a lot where he was comfortable in the early part of his career. But then we got under center a little more over the years, to help our running game and help our play-action game. I think that probably helped him a lot as he went to the NFL, just being under center and getting comfortable doing that. But it helped us use the tight ends, get us into more one-on-one situations. It was something he embraced, and it was good for us and for him in the long run. You see a lot of quarterbacks nowadays coming from pure spread systems in college who struggle to make the adjustment to getting under center when they get to the NFL because they've never done that before, they have not been in a pro-style offense before. So it helped us, and it helped him, too.

His sophomore year, his numbers actually dropped down statistically, on paper, and I think there were people who were disappointed, but to me, he played so much better that year. He really grew up as a quarterback. Coming off your freshman year, when you make a splash and everyone thinks you're going to be unbelievable all the time, you have to deal with those expectations. And there were times as a sophomore he didn't play as well, but going through that and how he handled that, I think that set him up for the year he had as a junior. You didn't see the improvements on paper, but as a coach, you saw it, you saw how he was handling things and leading his team. He was able to mature, so by his third year, he was ready. His first game that year, it was a big game, the opener against Iowa, on national TV, and he goes out and throws four interceptions. He went into the press conference and stood in front of the cameras and took all the blame for it. When I saw him do that, I knew he had matured. He came back and helped us win thirteen in a row. He grew a lot, not just physically, but maturity-wise.

Warren Moon

After his playing days, Moon did some work with agent Leigh Steinberg, taking quarterbacks who were preparing for the draft and helping to guide them through the process. In 2003, he spent the spring working with Roethlisberger and found him to be curious about the mental aspects of quarterbacking in the NFL.

WORKED WITH BEN and his quarterbacks coach at the time, Steve Clarkson. I went to as many of his workouts as I could, and I tried to lend my expertise as much as I could to him. What I liked about him is that mostly he wanted to just talk. He was really interested in what it took to be a professional, the transition into the game, the speed of the game, the things you would need to know once you got to a team and had to play and succeed. I knew Ben was going to be a great player when I saw him because here was this guy who was a big, physical specimen and if you saw him, you would not even think he was a quarterback. But when I watched him work out, you would never know he could do all the things he could do at that size. The thing that impressed me, physically, was the different throws he could make with his arm, he could throw the deep ball, he could throw to the sidelines, over the middle. He could make all the throws even then, before the draft. I remember being with him at Miami when he had a pro day for scouts, and watching all the scouts and coaches. It was obvious they liked what they were watching.

The Steelers took their time developing him once he started playing, before they gave him the full range. That was the best way to develop him, not giving him the whole playbook right away, not making him the guy who had to carry the football team. Just let him feel his way into the game, rely on that great running game and that defense, let him feel his way through. It is similar to what Seattle did with Russell Westbrook his first few years. He put the time in. They did not make things difficult for him. I thought the way they developed him was perfect, and you can see the results now with the way he is able to throw the ball, the confidence he has in himself and the confidence that team has in him.

Shane Montgomery

Before the 2004 draft, Roethlisberger was expected to be a top-10 pick, but as draft day neared, it became obvious that only two teams with top-10 picks—the Chargers, who had the No. 1 pick, and the Giants, who had No. 4—were angling for quarterbacks. Roethlisberger was among the top prospects, but several teams had him behind Phillip Rivers and Eli Manning on their draft boards. The Steelers, with the No. 11 pick, were hoping to land one of the three, having moved on from the short-lived Kordell Stewart era and looking to upgrade from Tommy Maddox. The Chargers and Giants wound up choosing Manning and Rivers, then swapping the two, allowing Roethlisberger to slide to the Steelers at No. 11. But those around Roethlisberger, including Montgomery, his offensive coordinator, knew he was close to being a Giant.

OBVIOUSLY, PHILLIP RIVERS and Eli were coming out at the same time. They were seniors and Ben came out a year early. You get close to a guy when you work with him, of course, so I was maybe biased, but I would have taken him over any quarterback in the country. I just thought he was that good. Terry Hoeppner, our head coach, was with him at the draft. And he thought the Giants were going to take him, I talked to him about that and his feeling was it would be the Giants. They'd had a lot of correspondence with the Giants, but they wound up taking Phillip and making the trade with San Diego. But when the Giants took Phillip and did that, after that, it was not certain what was going to happen, because there were a few teams in a row that were not looking for quarterbacks.

But he wound up in a great situation, with a stable franchise. Obviously, Tommy Maddox got hurt so he had to play a lot early in his career, but he won 14 straight games in his rookie year—he was ready to play. That was just the confidence he had about him, he was confident that he could be put in that situation and still do well. I always thought he had a chance. You never know if a guy is going to be a Hall of Fame–type quarterback, and you did not know how quickly he was going to get a chance to play in the league, you just never know that kind of thing. But he took advantage of his opportunity.

Mark Brunell

Brunell has seen the arc of Roethlisberger's career, from his ninth career start in 2004, while Brunell was a backup with Washington, through Roethlisberger's fourth AFC Championship game, a win over the Jets (for whom Brunell was also a backup) in January 2011.

HE'S VERY CONSISTENT. Year in and year out. Ben is at the point where you know he is going to produce and be productive, even when he has injuries or he doesn't have quite as much talent as usual. You know Ben is going to find a way to put up big numbers and win games. What I like most about Ben, and you saw this even when he was a young player, if the game is close and they are behind, he is going to be one of those quarterbacks who gives you a chance no matter the circumstances. Tom Brady, Aaron Rodgers, guys like that. Ben Roethlisberger has been one of those guys since the beginning of his career. He is tough, he is competitive. For a big guy like he is, he is very elusive and he can extend plays. You look at him and you don't think he is all that athletic, but he is. He is very tough to bring down.

CHAPTER 17

SUPER BOWL XL: PROMISE FULFILLED

Roethlisberger entered training camp in 2004 as the third-string quarterback behind Tommy Maddox and Charlie Batch. But Batch injured his knee in camp, and in the second game of his rookie season, Roethlisberger watched as Maddox, too, got hurt, injuring his elbow in a disastrous 30-13 loss to Baltimore. Roethlisberger was supposed to be brought along slowly, but he entered the Week 2 game with his team down, 20-0, in the third quarter and looked shaky at times. For Pittsburghers, panic had set in. Columnist Ron Cook wrote, "There's no way to soften the loss of Tommy Maddox yesterday. ... The Steelers' season is finished." Cook predicted, "The Steelers will be lucky to finish 5-11 without Maddox."

He was off by a country mile. Roethlisberger won his first start the following week in Miami and closed the season with 13 straight wins as a starter, the Steelers winning a 14th straight while resting their starters in the finale. Their 15-1 record was the best in AFC history and Roethlisberger won Rookie of the Year. The Steelers' year, though, finished in disappointment, as the team lost to the Patriots in the AFC championship game, their second loss in four years to New England with a trip to the Super Bowl on the line. After the game, Roethlisberger was distraught and felt especially bad for running back Jerome Bettis, who was turning 33 the following month and was considering retirement. Roethlisberger promised Bettis if he came back for the 2005 season, the Steelers would win the Super Bowl. (He later dubbed that "the dumbest promise I ever made.")

Dumb, perhaps. But prescient.

Marcellus Wiley

Wiley was in Dallas in 2004 and faced Ben Roethlisberger in just his third NFL start, then saw him again when he was with Jacksonville the following year. While most were surprised by Roethlisberger's sudden success, Wiley had been impressed when he met Ben months earlier.

I MET HIM AT Super Bowl before the draft (in 2004), and we were talking about being from a small school—I went to Columbia, he went to Miami, Ohio. So we were talking small-school, and it was funny, we were hanging out, partying and doing all the events, and it was cool because I got to see him before the lights got him. I always had respect for his disposition and how he was going to approach the game, how serious he was going to be about his craft. It obviously paid off.

The thing about Roethlisberger, you just don't expect a guy with that size, that girth, to be able to be so nimble. When you see it on film, it was almost hilarity. He was the king of taking three or four steps, but his three or four steps put more distance between him and other guys and caused more guys to miss sacks or quarterback hits than anybody else we saw on film. It was amazing that you could put him in a phone booth with a fly and he would not let the fly touch him. One thing I noticed about him, because I missed many sacks on him—I missed sacks in Jacksonville, I missed sacks in Dallas on him—the guy, when you get to him, it's almost as if he is playing in a DVR. He's like, OK, here you come, keep pushing, about to sack him. And he hits pause on the DVR, takes a look at you, he assesses you, and he just does a shoulder shrug real quick. You're going in fast-forward, he is in pause, and he is seeing it as slow as you can see it. Almost still motion. It's like diagnosing you. That's where people see him with that calm and poise. So many times I had that kill shot, and all he does is shoulder shrug, all he does is one-step. And you're like, 'This big old dude just figured me out so fast?' Just a tremendous level of poise and clarity in critical moments.

Cooper Carlisle
Offensive Lineman

Teams: Denver Broncos, 2000-06; Oakland Raiders, 2007-12

The Broncos thought they'd gotten lucky. The Steelers had been a good team in 2005, finishing 11-5, but they were a No. 6 seed, far from the 15-1 juggernaut they appeared to be the previous year. The most-feared team in the AFC that year was the Colts, who finished 14-2 and held the No. 1 seed in the conference. The Broncos had easily dispatched New England in their first playoff game, on a Saturday, and fully expected to be preparing for a trip to Indianapolis as they settled in to watch the Colts play the 8.5-point underdog Steelers. But Pittsburgh built a 21-3 lead, then was able to hold off a fourth-quarter rally that ended with a potential tying field goal missed by Colts kicker Mike Vanderjagt for a 21-18 Steelers win.

That set up a trip to Denver for the Steelers for the AFC Championship game. Once there, the Steelers romped, moving the ball easily in the first half and establishing a 24-3 halftime lead on a one-yard run by Bettis at the two-minute warning and a touchdown pass to Hines Ward with 15 seconds to go in the half that followed a Jake Plummer interception. For Broncos guard Cooper Carlisle, playing with an early lead only made the Steelers' defense all the more imposing.

WE WERE HAPPY they beat Indianapolis. Any time you can host a playoff game, it's great. But it wasn't like we thought, 'Oh, we have got a gimme game now that we don't have to play the Colts.' We knew the Steelers were a tough team and that it would be a challenge going against them. But we saw that game in Indy and, yeah, we were happy. We felt like we had a good chance to go to the Super Bowl. But we got behind in that game. They came in and they had won some games on the road, so getting behind makes it tough because those guys were able to pin their ears back and just sort of go. They were able to take some more risks. They scored two touchdowns at the end of the first half and that was really deflating, because I remember feeling like we were kind of fighting an uphill battle most of that game after that. We had a good running game, but we were not able to use it because we were trying to get back into the game.

Obviously, they had a ton of talent, that defense was really good. What I remember most is that Troy Polamalu was the best player on the field. You always had to know where he was, and he could be anywhere, they moved him around so much and he was a really smart, smart player. He would be making plays all over the place. He gambled a lot, as a lot of guys do. But with him, the gamble almost always seemed to pay off. He was unbelievable. They had tons of guys in front of him, James Farrior, Joey Porter, Casey Hampton, all of those guys, so the talent level was high. That front seven was so good, they sort of allowed Polamalu to run around and take chances.

I always had a ton of respect for Casey Hampton, especially in that defense, he played the nose so well. Did exactly what he was supposed to do, hard to move in the run game and hard to reach. He was just so heavy, like, not fat but solidly heavy and dense. Our zone-blocking system in Denver was more of a lateral thing, and he was very good at dealing with that. It was not just like he was a plugger, just a big body who filled up space like you get with some nose tackles. He could move, it was tough to get around him. He was a good player, not just a man-1 guy, just kind of took up space.

Their 3-4, schematically, is different. In our zone-blocking scheme, you still have all your run game stuff in, but it is an adjustment in how you get to the guy you're going to basically. For all those years, you knew they were going to be tough, they were going to be prepared, they were going to be consistent. They would always have a few kind of exotic blitzes in there. You knew what you were going to get in the 3-4, but they were going to give you those exotic blitzes and that is where they could make big plays on you.

The Steelers' surprising ride from the disappointment of the 2004 AFC Championship game, to Roethlisberger's promise to Bettis, to three road wins as the No. 6 seed in the 2005 season's playoffs finally stopped at Super Bowl XL in Detroit—fittingly, Bettis's hometown. It would be Pittsburgh's sixth Super Bowl appearance, and the first in the 30-year history of their opponents, the Seahawks. That storyline, along with Bettis's swan song and a bout of pregame trash talk between Pittsburgh linebacker Joey Porter and Seattle tight end Jerramy Stevens, dominated the run-up to the game.

Mack Strong

Running Back

Team: *Seattle Seahawks, 1994-2007*

Strong, who now runs the Mack Strong Foundation in Seattle, remains one of the great fullbacks in NFL history and played fourteen seasons for Seahawks. He rushed the ball all of 17 times and had only 22 catches in the 2005 season but earned a Pro Bowl slot for his work opening holes for league MVP Shaun Alexander.

JUST FIRST, BEING in a Super Bowl at all is a great experience. I describe it to people as the difference between riding in first class and riding in coach. I felt like, going to the Super Bowl, it is first class all the way. You are one of two teams still playing, so every article that gets written, everything that is said on ESPN or whatever networks, it is about you and your game and what you are about to do. Seahawks and Steelers. You have a different spring in your step in practice, even though you have played all these games and you're battered and bruised, but you don't feel it as much. You're one game away from being a world champion. That was my sentiment.

They had history on their side and everyone in the media was talking about that, but I didn't think it mattered. Every angle on every story it seemed like was the fact that it was the first Super Bowl in history for the Seahawks, and they had won four. For us, I think we looked at it like the history does not affect us. Where it was different, though, was on game day. Detroit is like an hour flight from Pittsburgh. There were probably 60,000 Steeler fans there, and about 10,000 Seahawks fans. It definitely felt like a home game for them, an away game for us. That was the only time—I stepped out onto that field and I was like, 'This is different.' It was supposed to be neutral. But we were just building our fan base at the time, and the Steelers, of course, had 30 or 40 years of winning and history behind them. It was weird walking into a neutral stadium and literally trying to figure out, 'Wait, where are our fans at?'

Walter Jones

Offensive Lineman

Team: Seattle Seahawks, 1997-2008

Walter Jones was a star left tackle from his arrival in Seattle, where he played twelve seasons and earned nine Pro Bowl selections and was inducted into the Hall of Fame in 2014. He listened with some bemusement as Jerramy Stevens went back and forth with Joey Porter, who said of Stevens, "This guy is almost a first-round bust who barely made some plays this year." Jones knew that the more worked up Porter got, the more he would be seeing of him on the left side of the line—along with Kimo von Oelhoffen and his well-known club move.

I KNEW GOING INTO that week, they were hyping up that game as Jerome Bettis's last game, it being in his hometown and all of that stuff. There was a lot said about it, and everyone was saying it was going to be a home game for Pittsburgh and all of that. That was it, Jerramy said something about Jerome not winning, and Joey Porter sort of went off on him in a media conference. So going into the game, that week, Joey and Jerramy Stevens got into the little bickering and talking and stuff. At that point, I was looking forward to the matchup, because he was going back and forth with Jerramy and I was thinking, he is going to do all this talking and stuff.

I had Joey a lot. Joey was tough to play against. But he was pretty quiet for most of the game actually. All of a sudden, he made a play, there was one play when Jerramy made a block on him and he started jawing. That got Joey all fired up. I had watched him on TV all week, so I thought he would be talking *all* game, but it was really that, he just needed that button to be pushed. Joey uses his mouth as part of his game, and it took only one or two plays during the game before he got into it and was jawing. I think one of their coaches had to kind of come in and calm things down for him, tell him not to say anything but during the game at first I think he was focused and didn't say much. But it took one block and that woke him up. He did not say anything to me but once that block happened, he started jawing, and I think it added motivation to him, to say, 'OK, this is what I needed,' and he got focused there.

Their lineman, No. 67, I can't always remember his name (Kimo von Oelhoffen), but I just remember his club move. He played the

4-technique and, man, he used that club technique every time on me, and I was thinking, 'Man, this guy is trying to knock my head off every time.' He was pretty good at that and I had to make adjustments to him as the game went on. This guy was pretty strong. This guy was so good, I watched him all year, that was his move—he had the outside step and come back with the club move. Some guys he could club and club right across the body, but I was prepared for that club. But he was doing it all game and I just, when I got done with that game, my body was so sore from him doing that club move. I knew from that game, we had prepared for it, because he was pretty effective with that club move.

We were going to go out and do the things we were going to do all year. We were a short-pass team, we would throw the ball short and the receivers would make plays—the dink-and-dunk as they called it, that kind of offense. We had gotten pretty good at that offense with Matt Hasselbeck, he knew how to run that offense and we knew what we wanted to do to those guys. They had those guys on the defensive line, that is where it starts for them, but we had a really good offensive line and we felt like we could open some holes for Shaun Alexander like we had been all year. But that was the one thing that got us behind the eight ball was that we could not get the ball running and moving on the ground the way we usually did the entire season. Their defense was stout, they were pretty good, too, of course. They were coming in as the No. 6 seed, winning on the road, so they were feeling pretty good about themselves.

Mack Strong

One of the critical plays in Super Bowl XL wound up taking place early, with the Seahawks driving deep into Steelers territory with 2:08 to play in the first quarter. Quarterback Matt Hasselbeck found Darrell Jackson in the end zone for what appeared to be a 16-yard touchdown—until a flag came in and Jackson was whistled for a pass interference penalty on safety Chris Hope. The Seahawks were forced to settle for a field goal on the drive.

I **HAVE SEEN THE** replay. I think that is one of those calls, half the time it gets called, half the time it gets ignored. I didn't think it was anything where he gained an advantage but there is a little bit in there where you can see, OK, that is where the flag came from. But having said that, you just, usually in the Super Bowl the referees let them play. That's my sentiment on that.

Walter Jones

From Jones's perspective, the missed chance at a touchdown sapped momentum from a Seahawks offense that relied on getting into and maintaining a groove.

AS A LINEMAN you don't see the whole play but I looked up and saw a touchdown. Then you see the flag and you look at the replay and the ref made the call. I thought it was one of those calls that was a decision by the referee that you don't have to make. I thought the cornerback did a good acting job, but the referee had to make the call. I don't want it to come off as sour grapes, but of course you are going to be biased toward your own team. At that point, as a lineman, you are blocking and fighting for your life, and you look up and think he has a touchdown. That hurt a little because we were a rhythm team and we wanted to get into a rhythm but we never got a chance to get into that rhythm and start feeling good about our offense. The Steelers defense was too good not to take advantage of opportunities. That sort of set the tone.

In that game it was. We had some dropped balls in that game that were really what the coaches called drive-killers. They were plays that hurt drives, they were dropped balls, and then there were the penalties. But those moments, you are playing a game and you figure out what you are doing wrong during a season, you try to correct the stuff you are bad at and become better at the stuff you are good at. It is a long season and you work on that, but you have one game where you lose concentration and that is where that stuff comes back up and it comes back strong. With us, penalties and dropped balls, those came up all over again. It was a situation where if you make those plays, it could have been a different game. We had opportunities but we just let them get away and you don't get those back.

Even with the tough call against Jackson, and a 54-yard missed field goal by kicker Josh Brown, the Steelers were up just 7-3 on the Seahawks at halftime. But the second turning point in the game took place on the Steelers' second play of the second half, just 10 seconds after the teams resumed action. Running back Willie Parker took a handoff and bolted through the right side of the line, surprised to see a wide-open hole in front of him. Parker accelerated through and ran 75 yards for a touchdown and a 14-3 lead without even being touched by a Seahawk. Seattle did come back to pull within 14-10 after a Roethlisberger interception, but the Steelers delivered a fourth-quarter dagger when Antwaan Randle El hit Hines Ward on a reverse pass for a 43-yard touchdown.

Mack Strong

As a fullback, Strong appreciated a good hole through the defensive line, but he was surprised to see the Steelers give Parker as much space as he got.

TO GET ONE right up the gut? Untouched for 75 yards? Yeah, that is every running back's dream. He is a speedy guy of course, so once he gets past the second level, it is kind of a done deal. But at that time, one of our best players, our top safety—Marquand Manuel—had gotten hurt and was out. That was something that, maybe that play doesn't happen if he is there. He was really good at making tackles in space and reading the play. He was a big reason why we didn't give up a whole lot of big plays. We had another guy, Rocky Bernard, who had a fumble return or an interception return, and he pulled a hamstring. He was done for the rest of that game. Some goofy things happened in that game, and you look at it like, 'Man!' Not taking anything away from the Steelers and what a good team they were, but we just felt like we did not play our best.

On the defensive side, all year, we had been good at just not giving up big plays, explosive plays. We gave up two in that game. I think of the reverse pass for a touchdown to Hines Ward, and I think about the long, 75-yard run from Willie Parker, which I think is still a Super Bowl record. You just look at those two plays, and you take those out, and maybe we give ourselves an opportunity. But like I said, we just didn't play the way we had played all year, and it is really disappointing to know that.

Walter Jones

Jones and the offensive line were busy on the sideline preparing for the second half and didn't get a look at Parker's run until he heard the crowd.

IT WAS ONE of those situations where, if you're an offensive lineman, you don't watch that part of the game as much. But it was good for us for a while because it seemed like they were in the same position that we were, they were not feeling comfortable in their offense, either. I mean it was a low score at halftime (7-3, Pittsburgh) and we were just coming out for the second half and then you look up and all of a sudden, they have that one play. We were going over our adjustments and then it was just, 'Uh-oh, something happened.' That really sparked everything for them. That gave them the momentum, that was the play that put them in the driver's seat. Our defense was playing pretty good, holding them up and keeping us in the game, giving us opportunities. But one play and that's it, it changes the game, and we go down, 14-3.

Overall, the Seahawks outgained the Steelers, 396 yards to 339. They forced two Steelers turnovers and felt that the game was played at their pace. But several dropped passes and seven penalties proved fatal, and Roethlisberger, Parker, Ward and Co. did just enough to secure the 21-10 win and send Bettis out with a Super Bowl ring.

Mack Strong

Shaun Alexander wound up with 20 carries in the game, while the Seahawks threw the ball 49 times—to Strong that was not nearly enough balance. And when, four years after Super Bowl XL, referee Bill Leavy publicly apologized to the Seahawks because he "kicked two calls in the fourth quarter," there was not a lot of consolation.

I DIDN'T FEEL LIKE we ran the ball enough. We had the league MVP, Shaun Alexander, we had the best offensive line in football and we only ran the ball 20 times. We tried to throw it a bunch, but that wasn't our identity that year. So I think we got away from some of the things that we had done throughout the whole year. All that said, it was a real lost opportunity to come up with a win in that game. Overall, I look at that game as kind of a missed opportunity to be honest with you. There were circumstances around that game that, in most Super Bowl games, in most championship games, you don't see as many flags. Especially, I think more toward one team than the other. There is a lot about the calls in that game, but I look at that game and I still feel we did not play our best game.

I thought we could run the football on them. They had gotten in as the sixth seed, and had to go and win three games on the road to get to the Super Bowl. I know how hard it is to win playoff games on the road, or to win any game on the road. It takes a lot out of you. I felt like they were tired coming into that game. The Steelers have a reputation for having very physical defenses, linebackers, that kind of thing. I felt like if we could keep running the football, we had a chance to make that happen. But for whatever reason, we went away from it. We were in the huddle and we kept saying, 'OK, the next play is going to be the play.' We believed it, that we were about to break through.

The penalties, those are the things that add to the frustration when you are just trying to get back to your game plan. The call on Matt Hasselbeck (in the fourth quarter) when he got called for a chop block when he threw an interception. Why do you call that? They never call that. A couple years after, the referee came out and admitted that he kicked some calls. I didn't want to hear that. To me, that was just more salt in the wound. It was like, 'Duh, we know that.' But at the end of the day, as players out there on the field, you have to overcome that. Pittsburgh is a good team and they took advantage of all the opportunities we gave them.

Walter Jones

Walter Jones was elated to be chosen for the Hall of Fame and said he does not think about the Super Bowl XL loss much. But once it is brought up, he says, the memories come flooding back.

AFTER 10 YEARS, you know, that game comes right back to me. You can be talking to your friends or in the barbershop or something and someone will bring it up and you start talking about it and it comes right back to you and you remember all the defining plays that happened in that game. You can get different opinions about the game, about the calls, about the plays that happened, but for me, I just say, those are the things that happen in a game, you know? It's still tough sometimes. Coaches say they remember the losses more than the wins, and for players, you remember the bad plays more than the good plays. It is a loss that, in the end, we can say we had our chances, but credit to the Steelers, they won it.

Remember, we were in the Super Bowl for the first time. I think they were going for their fourth one, their fourth win. They had been in five of them before. They had Jerome Bettis retiring and there was a lot of stuff going on. That was my ninth year, it was tough, a tough game to lose. No one remembers the runners-up. You think about the victorious stuff you are going to do after the game, but you don't think about, dang, going into that losing locker room and everything is over. But that's how quickly things end. I think I have actually watched that game only twice. I thought it was just one of those rare games that, we were there but I don't think we were ready to win it all. I don't think we were ready, and the Steelers were.

CHAPTER 18

SUPER BOWL XLIII: CARDINAL CLASSIC

THREE YEARS AFTER their win in Super Bowl XL, the Steelers were again in familiar territory—they were 12-4 behind a suffocating defense that led the league in yardage and points allowed, the kind of numbers the old Steel Curtain gang would be proud of. But these Steelers were different. Back in January 2007, coach Bill Cowher resigned after 15 years as coach, eschewing the demands of head coaching in order to spend time with his family and get into broadcasting. That set off a two-week scramble in which the frontrunners for the job were believed to be assistant coaches Ken Whisenhunt and Russ Grimm. But when Whisenhunt was hired by Arizona, the Steelers shocked the league by going with 34-year-old Vikings coordinator Mike Tomlin, the first black coach in the franchise's history.

Tomlin was solid (10-6) in his first season as coach but had an outstanding second season, going 12-4. In the postseason, Tomlin's Steelers dispatched the Chargers in the divisional round, then prepared for the AFC Championship game against the team that had developed into their archenemy over the previous decade: the Baltimore Ravens.

Derrick Mason

Wide Receiver

Teams: Tennessee Titans, 1997-2004; Baltimore Ravens, 2005-10; New York Jets and Houston Texans, 2011

Derrick Mason played fifteen seasons in the NFL and went against the Steelers twenty-seven times in his career. But his most memorable games were the ones he played while with the Ravens, at the height of the Baltimore-Pittsburgh rivalry in the 2000s. Maybe the most important of those showdowns came in January 2009, when the Steelers edged past the Ravens and second-year quarterback Joe Flacco in the AFC Championship game at Heinz Field—a game best remembered for Troy Polamalu's late interception returned for a touchdown that sealed a 23-14 win.

IT WAS JOE'S second year. You know, he was going to make some mistakes, he had shown a lot during the season but it was his first year. He was a rookie at Heinz Field playing for the AFC Championship and it was maybe 10 or 15 degrees and kind of windy and just a cold, cold day. We got to Pittsburgh and they just made it so difficult on Joe, especially in the second half. They came with every blitz imaginable, they would change up their coverage and try their best to confuse him. Whatever they were doing, it seemed like it worked. The Steelers had a really good team, but we just thought, this is our opportunity to dethrone Pittsburgh. I truly believe that if, with that team, that was Joe's third or fourth year, we win hands down. I just think they threw stuff at us that would be trouble for any quarterback, you could be 10 years in the league. But they were throwing stuff at us with a second-year quarterback.

The X-factor was always Troy. He always managed to have his best games against us. I think he got up for the rivalry as much as we did. There was a lot of hate going around that field. You did not know whether Troy was blitzing, whether he was covering, whether he was coming up to help on the run. I mean the guy, he was allowed to roam the field and I think that was the only guy on that defense who had all the freedom in the world. We had a fourth-and-1 play, fourth-and-inches, really, and we were running a sneak all the way. Troy went up to the line of scrimmage, jumped over the line and grabbed Joe and pulled him back. He was always doing things that you would say, 'Wait now, how did he do that?' You had to account for where he was at all times. If you didn't, one minute he would be on the line of scrimmage coming through and getting a sack, the next minute he would be back at the line of scrimmage, but then he would drop back to the middle of the field and get into coverage and mess you up that way, because he had such good range.

The interception was just difficult. We had the ball, it was third and long and that place was loud, they were going crazy. It was only two points (16-14) so we just had to get to field-goal range. The play call was to me, we needed something like 12 yards. Joe was looking toward me and I just saw Troy get into the passing lane and jump and make the play. He just read it, that was what he did so well and like I say, if Joe had more experience he might have been able to look him off and then come back to me. Troy got underneath and when Joe threw the pass, he jumped it and ran it in. You always had to know where Troy was, and we didn't on that play.

Troy was key, because Pittsburgh never prided themselves on having shutdown corners. That was not part of their defense really. Ike Taylor was pretty good in his prime. But they were never going to play press, man-to-man the whole game. They were not going to put their corners in that situation. They did a lot of zone blitzing, they were going to put their corners in a position to succeed. They covered up for their corners. It was their front seven that did the most for those guys. But even that game, I think that was the game where I was going over the middle and Lawrence Timmons just gave me a big hit. I have taken a lot of hits from Pittsburgh Steelers linebackers, but that is one I still remember.

With the Ravens behind then, the storyline heading into Super Bowl XLIII was familiar faces. The NFC champs, the Cardinals, had slipped into the playoffs only by winning a poor NFC West division with a 9-7 record, but that marked part of a steady improvement under a rebuilding plan that made Arizona look eerily recognizable to Steeler fans: there were 11 members of the team and coaching staff that had spent time in Pittsburgh, notably head coach Ken Whisenhunt and assistant head coach Russ Grimm, the two finalists to replace Bill Cowher for the head-coaching job that went to Mike Tomlin. Offensive coordinator Todd Haley had grown up in Pittsburgh and was a ball boy for the Steelers dynasty teams of the 1970s—his father, Dick Haley, was a former defensive back for Pittsburgh and was the Steelers' personnel director who drafted the likes of Jack Ham, Franco Harris, and the famed 1974 class that included Hall of Famers Lynn Swann, Jack Lambert, John Stallworth, and Mike Webster. It was little wonder the Cardinals were known as Pittsburgh West.

The Cardinals had lost four out of their final six regular-season games, but their offense kicked in during the playoffs, scoring 31.7 points per game, behind quarterback Kurt Warner and a trio of receivers—Larry Fitzgerald, Anquan Boldin, and Steve Breaston—who all had more than 1,000 yards, just the fifth time in league history that feat had been accomplished. But anchored by Pro Bowl linebackers James Farrior and James Harrison, as well as Polamalu, the Steelers were the best defense in the NFL, leading the league in yards (3,795, the only team to hold opponents under 4,000 yards) and points allowed, and finishing second in sacks.

A great offense on one side, a great defense on the other. They wound up producing one of the best Super Bowls in history.

Mike Miller
Coach

Mike Miller had worked in Pittsburgh from 1999 to 2003, his first job in football, and went on to join the Arizona staff in 2007 as the wide receivers coach. He was working with that top-tier group in the Cardinals' Super Bowl season, and it was clear that taking advantage of their skills would be vital to beating a Pittsburgh team Miller knew well.

TO BE HONEST with you, we thought we could attack their secondary. I thought they had a Hall of Fame safety in Troy Polamalu, and he was, in my opinion, the greatest strong safety to play the game, I think he revolutionized the position. But the other three, I think they were average players. The other guy we felt we were worried about was Deshea Townsend. Deshea played at Alabama and we thought he was a heck of a player. But we were not really impressed with the other guys in the secondary. The Steelers built that defense the way they built all their defenses throughout their history, which was they had a front seven that was in the Top 3—every year, it seems, their front seven is in the top 3 in every category. They're physical, they're fast. They had Casey Hampton anchoring the middle, who was just such a great anchor for that 3-4, he would dominate the inside and he was so athletic. And a smart guy, he could run, amazing athlete, could flow to the ball. They had Aaron Smith on that unit, very strong, very powerful, great with his hands, almost impossible to get movement on. Their theory was, we're going to get to you before you can expose our secondary. So you had Casey, James Harrison, Larry Foote and there was Troy behind them. They knew what their strength was.

And of course, there was LaMarr Woodley on the right side at linebacker and James Harrison on the other side—Harrison was the defensive MVP that year. James was really in his prime. I scouted

James when he was at Kent State and told the Steelers to sign him when he went undrafted. Tim Gribble was our scouting director and he told me, if you are going out there, you better keep an eye on him. You could just tell right away, the guy was just tough. When I was coaching in Buffalo, James got a sack-fumble against us to go to the playoffs, and he winds up making one of the biggest plays in the game against us in the Super Bowl. So, yeah, I am really glad I told the Steelers to sign him.

Inside they had James Farrior, and to me, he was one of the most unsung players anywhere, because he was so smart. He was physical, but the difference was, he just prepared with such detail, a great leader, could fly to the ball, great at defending the pass as well as the run. I had great respect for him. Larry Foote was another guy—a tough player, but a really smart guy, too. Every year, you look at them, and they have so many smart guys, they're so well coached.

Clancy Pendergast
Defensive Coordinator

On the other side of the ball, defensive coordinator Clancy Pendergast—a holdover after coach Ken Whisenhunt arrived from Pittsburgh—liked the way his defense had taken shape in the playoffs but had major concerns with Ben Roethlisberger and wide receiver Santonio Holmes, who had gone for 70 yards and a touchdown in the AFC Championship game.

THOSE 11 STARTERS had been with me for four or five years, so it was a pretty veteran group. There was never any doubt, the confidence in our defense and the players we had. You're talking about

Bertrand Berry, Antonio Smith, Karlos Dansby, Darnell Dockett, Antrel Rolle, those are guys who I had coached and grew up with in that system. We had a chip on our shoulder that Arizona had not been in the position to play in the playoffs a lot. With the way our offense was scoring that year, they were scoring points in such bunches that year, the strategy a lot of teams had was to slow things down and try to run it on us, keep the offense off the field. We knew the goal was to stop the run and keep offenses from hitting those big plays on us.

You've got to stop the run first, and if you can do that, you have to deal with Ben Roethlisberger and how you are going to handle him, the broken plays that he makes, those are the most dangerous ones. Santonio Holmes, we felt like he was a big part of their offense, that we wanted to focus on taking him out of the game as much as we could, match him up as much as we could with Dominique Rodgers-Cromartie, who was a rookie that year but he was about the only guy we had who could run with Santonio Holmes. We were going to match him up with him and do some things to protect him, but we knew we were going to have to play some 1-on-1 coverages to where they were matched up. We couldn't sacrifice playing single-high to stop the run all the time, we would have to protect the passing game as well. We had our hands full.

When you watch their games, a lot of plays Ben made were loose plays. A lot of their games came down to the end that season—and even if you watch him now—that is probably when he is at his best. Leading up to that week, those two weeks before the Super Bowl, that was something we practiced more than anything defensively, the 2-minute drill. You're playing in a game like that, I knew, there was a good chance it was going to come down to the last two minutes of the game. We wanted to be overly prepared for that, because it is obviously the biggest game of your life. We played them in 2007 in Arizona and had to stop Roethlisberger at the end of the game to win at our place, and we were able to do it.

The Steelers employed the theory that a slow, steady offense was the best way to limit Arizona's explosive passing game, and in the first quarter, Pittsburgh opened with a five-minute drive that led to a field goal, then notched a drive that chewed up the final 6:13 of the first quarter and produced a touchdown early in the second quarter. The Cardinals ran just six plays in the first quarter. But Arizona responded with a touchdown pass from Warner to tight end Ben Patrick to make the score 10-7, and when Karlos Dansby intercepted a pass from Roethlisberger deep in Pittsburgh territory with 2:09 to play in the first half, the Cardinals were poised for a momentum-changing score.

But the momentum would go to the black and gold. Warner drove the Cardinals to the 1-yard line and, on first down with 18 seconds to play, fired a goal-line pass to Anquan Boldin. James Harrison bulled in front of Boldin, though, not only intercepting the pass but running 100 yards the other way for a Steelers touchdown. A potential 14-10 Cardinals lead at halftime instead became a 17-7 Steelers lead.

Mike Miller

Harrison's interception was especially disappointing to the Cardinals because they thought they'd recognized a potential problem in that pass pattern but fixed it. Harrison, though, still made the play.

THE MISTAKE WITH the interception return or mistakes that would not be obvious from just watching the game. You wish you didn't make those mistakes.

There are some things that took place that we were aware of before the play. We tried to get it corrected. As we read the play, James

Harrison was supposed to blitz. But James apparently thought that was a mistake, so rather than blitz, he dropped at the last second, we did not think he would be there. He was able to step in and make a play on the ball. Then, we just had missed tackles the other way and he was able to go 100 yards for a touchdown.

Clancy Pendergast

Pendergast was satisfied that his defense had put the Cardinals in position to score with the interception, and as Arizona got to the 1-yard line, he was preparing for the second half.

THE TOUCHDOWN AT the end of the half, we were sitting pretty good just before that. Karlos Dansby got the interception, and we got the ball back for our offense. They drove down and then the interception happened, and that took seven points off the board for us, put seven up for them. It was eye-popping to me. I was talking to our guys on the sideline, getting through some adjustments we were making, things we were going to talk about at halftime. I heard the crowd roar and I figured we scored. But I looked up and there they are running down the sideline, we're trying to tackle him and no one can get him down for 100 yards. But our guys bounced back, they were a resilient group.

Trailing 20-7 in the fourth quarter, Warner rallied his team, leading an eight-play, 87-yard drive, during which he completed eight straight passes. With a little more than three minutes to play in the game, the Steelers were backed up to their 1-yard line after an unnecessary roughness penalty. On a third-and-10, Pittsburgh was whistled for a holding penalty in the end zone, which cut the deficit to 20-16 and gave the Cardinals a safety and the ball back. On their second play after the safety, Cardinals star receiver Larry Fitzgerald cut inside for on a mid-range route, took a pass from Warner, and bolted 64 yards for a touchdown.

Mike Miller

The Fitzgerald touchdown—his second of the day, to go with his 127 yards receiving—remains one of the most memorable plays from Super Bowl XLIII. Miller said it was a route the Cardinals put in after watching the Colts beat the Steelers back in Week 10 of the regular season.

THAT WAS A good play that we had put in knowing at the time that the Steelers liked to play 2-man. We call that an 'under' concept. It is actually something we stole off the Indianapolis Colts watching them throughout the year. But the slot receiver pushes up 10-12 yards, we call that a 'Do It.' If he has a man inside at 12 yards, he can break out. Larry comes up behind and is pushing up at five yards and he is breaking in, and that is an under route. Give credit to Kurt Warner, because he got right to the line and recognized the coverage and made the call. He saw it, and when Anquan, running a 'Do It,' broke out, both safeties went with him and Kurt saw it, got it to Larry doing the under route, and that is why there was no one in the middle of the field. Larry just took it between the hashes, there was no safety help, and Larry hit the afterburners.

Larry had done pretty well against Ike Taylor in his career, and I think he knew, especially at that point in his career, that he felt good about every matchup he had. He is a Hall of Famer in every way, the details he prepares with. But we felt that they did not have enough defensive backs to cover all three, so it was, pick your poison. If you took Larry and Anquan out, Steve could beat you. If you were in man on Larry, he was going to beat you. Breaston had six catches in that game, and he was our third receiver. We felt like there were still plenty of plays left out there on the field that, for one reason or another, we didn't get the ball there. But a lot of credit goes to them for that.

After the Fitzgerald score, Pittsburgh got the ball back with two timeouts, trailing, 23-20, with 2:30 to play. That was when Roethlisberger and receiver Santonio Holmes came alive. Roethlisberger found Holmes on a third-and-6 from his own 26-yard line for a first down with 1:56 to play. Then, with 1:02 to play and the ball at the Cardinals 46-yard line, Roethlisberger pump-faked to running back Mewelde Moore in the flat, then zipped a 10-yard pass to Holmes near the right sideline. As safety Aaron Francisco slipped to the turf, Holmes turned to the outside and raced to the Cardinals 6-yard line. On first down from the six, the Cardinals dodged a bullet when a blown coverage left Holmes open in the left corner, but Roethlisberger missed him. The Steelers went back to the play, though, in the right corner on second down, and this time, Roethlisberger and Holmes connected to give the Steelers a rousing 27-23 victory.

Clancy Pendergast

Pendergast had been telling his defense that Super Bowl XLIII almost certainly would come down to a drive in the final two minutes, and he was right. He detailed closely the two critical plays on the drive— Santonio Holmes's 40-yard catch-and-run, and the thought process he had as the Cardinals tried to keep the Steelers out of the end zone on a first-and-goal situation that wound up with Holmes making the game-winning touchdown catch.

WE HAD CONFIDENCE heading into that last drive. We had some bad breaks before that. But we had held them to about 200 total yards before that last drive, it was an 88-yard drive. So our guys had done what we set out to do. We had a lot of confidence in ourselves and how we were going to handle that last drive. There was a particular situation, the second play of the drive, and they threw it deep down the sideline. Aaron Francisco looked like he had an interception on the play, but the receiver (Nate Washington) was able to dislodge it from him. If you look from the end zone feed, you can see Karlos Dansby and Adrian Wilson with their hands up because they thought Aaron had it intercepted. That kept their drive alive.

On the big play to Santonio, they ran a curl and a flat combination, with the back (Mewelde Moore) and the X receiver. Ben wanted to throw the curl, the flat was open, but Chike Okeafor jumped it and got into his passing lane. Ben basically windmilled the ball like he does, and stepped up. Most guys, if you can throw the ball that hard, as hard as Ben does, it is going to come out of their hand when you windmill it. But he is strong, he held onto it and because Chike did such a good job jumping into his throwing lane, Ben held it longer and that altered Aaron's path to the No. 1 receiver, to Santonio. Aaron had a good angle on the play to start with, but once Ben reloaded and made that throw, it threw Aaron off and he lost his balance, he was left with a poor angle on the play, coming directly in. It makes it look like Aaron was the culprit more than he should be.

They were first-and-goal from the 8-yard line. I was on the sideline and you just try to keep your composure and get your guys to keep their composure. I figured, we hold them to three points, we are tied, we go into overtime. The plan was coverage on first down, coverage on second down, all-out blitz on third down, field-goal situation on fourth down. They ran a concept at that time that they had run earlier in the game. That was down at the other end of the field on a third-down play, and we had the same coverage on, but at that time, we did not play it correctly in our secondary and that route was open the first time. So we got it corrected. It was a man-type concept that went to zone based on alignment, so we tried to get it corrected on the sideline.

You watch 17 games on an offensive coordinator, you get a pretty good feel for how they're going to call a game. So I had a feeling that Coach (Bruce) Arians was going to go back to that play in this situation because they had success with it before. So we had the same coverage and we thought we had it corrected. But on first down, we left the seven-route—the corner route—open, and Ben just overthrew Santonio and it went through Santonio's hands in the corner. But it was there for them. Second down, rather than try that coverage again, we went to zone coverage in the end zone so it was basically a quarter, quarter, quarter, quarter, across the board, for each defensive back. They ran basically the same concept, except they flipped the formation, so Santonio was going to the right corner. The secondary played it the same way, and they jumped up on Hines Ward on the play and left the seven-route wide open. It should have been zoned off where the corner had the seven cut, the inside player had the receiver hooking up and somebody was in the flat. We just misplayed the route. It was disappointing in that respect. Santonio made a great catch, they got the touchdown, and you have to give all the credit to them.

I felt like, if we got them down to third down and we could all-out blitz them, where the ball was, we had a chance, that was our strength. If you blitz them on first and second down, they get the ball to the edge and you miss a tackle, the game is over. As a coordinator, you're always thinking of the scenarios, what they need, what is the situation, what's the best thing for our guys. As soon as we got down to the tight-red area, my thought process was zone, zone, then all-out blitz.

I have a hard time ever looking at it, to be honest with you. They ended up with more points than we did, but you learn from every experience. The one thing people don't talk about is when we had them backed up against their goal line and we all-out blitzed them and we got the safety and gave our offense the ball back. They score the touchdown to give us the lead with four minutes to go. That was, for me, one of the most memorable plays from that standpoint. We ended up bringing six guys, had a twist inside there, we felt like with our matchups, if we had some games going on with the pressure, that we would have an opportunity to make a play. That scenario came up and we executed it, and the refs made the right call.

I was fired after that Super Bowl. I guess it is kind of bittersweet. But people make decisions, they do what they do. I hold my head high about the way we played defense during my time in Arizona. Obviously, getting an opportunity to play the Steelers in a Super Bowl is a special opportunity but I would love to have a chance to get back there again.

Mike Miller

For Miller, who grew up a Steelers fan and had friends in the organization, the loss was bittersweet.

I **AM A LOYAL** guy and I go all in with the organization I am with. It is hard to move on after you build relationships with people, even though in the business, everybody moves around a lot. But I am from Pittsburgh, and when it is your ultimate dream to win the Super Bowl, to be able to do it against your hometown team, that is the ultimate. I used to wear a Terrible Towel like it was a cape. I mean, I knew all the rosters, every year, and I still do to this day. But I had worked there so I had still had close friends with the team, even then. I don't like playing against my friends, because every time you lose, you are one step closer to being fired. It is part of the job, and something you expect, but you never want to be the one who brings that on a friend. So in the end, I would rather play someone I never had any connection to, so you don't have to worry about it. But from a competitive side, it is the Steelers. It is the best franchise in the league. You want to measure yourself against the best and see what you can do. The Steelers were clearly that, they were the best.

Still, you see that logo, the Super Bowl logo, every year and I can't help but think about that game. It still leaves you with that empty kind of feeling. I am not one to say, 'Well, we played well, that's good enough.' It is so hard to put together the right plays to get a first down. Then it is so hard to put together a whole drive of plays and actually score a touchdown. Then just to win a game. But to put enough wins together to make the playoffs, win the division, win in the playoffs? It's really hard. So when you get to the Super Bowl you feel like you have got to win. Because you appreciate how hard it is. It was a thrill, but you want to win.

CHAPTER 19

"PART OF THEIR DNA"

IT CERTAINLY DID not appear as though 2010 held much promise for the Steelers, not when Ben Roethlisberger was handed a four-game NFL suspension tied to offseason sexual assault allegations (no charges were filed). That hopeless feeling was amplified in Week 1, when safety Troy Polamalu injured his knee, an injury that limited him to five games that season. But the Pittsburgh defense clamped down with the team missing its two stars, allowing just 12.3 points per game, and the combination of Charlie Batch and Dennis Dixon at quarterback played well enough to help the Steelers manage a 3-1 start. Roethlisberger returned to lead the Steelers to a 9-3 record the rest of the way, and he threw for 17 touchdowns and only five interceptions.

The Steelers postseason began with a known foe: the Ravens, against whom Pittsburgh had split its season series in a pair of taut defensive struggles, Baltimore winning 17-14 in the first game and Pittsburgh taking the second, 13-10. The Steelers pulled off a come-from-behind 31-24 win in the postseason against Baltimore and withstood a comeback effort from the Jets in the conference championship, 24-19. That put them, incredibly, into their eighth Super Bowl, and though they suffered a 31-25 loss to the Packers, the game itself was steeped in glory.

Derrick Mason

Once again, Mason and the Ravens went into the playoffs and found themselves looking at a date with the Steelers. Things looked good—finally—for Baltimore in the first half, as the Ravens defense had jumped on Roethlisberger and forced two fumbles, each of which led to Ravens touchdowns. A missed field goal by Pittsburgh helped Baltimore establish a 21-7 halftime lead before disaster struck.

IT HAS BEEN the best rivalry in football over the last 10, 15 years. I would call it a respectful hate. You knew that when you played the Steelers, you were going to get their best and their worst. Meaning they were going to come at you with all they had and they were going to do it borderline crossing that line, but they never did. There was no love lost, there was some hatred there, but there was respect there, too. Every year, the schedule would come out and we would circle it—Steeler week. It was always a focus for us. We were intense all the time, but on Steeler week, we made sure every *t* was crossed, every *i* was dotted, because you never wanted to be put in the position where they might embarrass you.

That game, we had them, they were down by double-digits at the half and we were just feeling like this was our year to beat them and go to the Super Bowl. We took it to them in the first half, we were getting after Roethlisberger, we had turnovers, everything was going our way. We were in Pittsburgh, but we had won in Pittsburgh that year, and they beat us at our place. But we came out at halftime, and we had the ball down in our own end and what happens? Fumble. Ray Rice fumbled it, inside our own 20, they run two plays, touchdown.

We get the ball back a little while later, what happens? Interception. Joe was trying deep for Todd Heap and kind of floated it and their safety was there. We give them the ball at maybe our 20 yard line, again. Three, four more plays later, touchdown. Now we are tied. We get the ball back, another fumble. Now we give up a field goal and we're down. Our defense was good, but as an offense, you can't put them in positions like that on the road in the playoffs. We gave them

17 points. That is deflating. To go to Heinz Field and be up, 21-7, to the Pittsburgh Steelers, there was no way we thought we were going to lose that game. No way. We thought we were going to the Super Bowl. We really did.

The big thing was, we tied it up in the fourth quarter (24-24 on a Billy Cundiff field goal) and they get the ball back with four minutes. You're just watching from the sideline, hoping that the defense can get a stop. Just never happened. That four-minute drill, the four-minute drive, it is sometimes more demoralizing than a two-minute drive. We felt pretty good. They had a third-and-19 right about two minutes to go, and we were getting ready like we were going back on the field. Get your helmet on. I don't think our defense gave up a third-and-19 that whole year. But then they throw it deep, and we give it up. And it wasn't anything crazy, it was just a go route to Antonio Brown on the right sideline. That was a heartbreaker right there.

But playing those guys was fun. I respect Mike Tomlin a lot. They were a team that prides themselves on their history, they were always well aware of it, their fans were well aware of it and even if they were not having their best year, they knew what a Pittsburgh Steeler is supposed to play like. Whether they were having a good season or not. They have had what, three coaches in 50 years? That speaks volumes. The organization is one of the most stable in all of sports. Not just football but all of sports.

Larry McCarren

McCarren was a twelve-year center for the Packers and earned two Pro Bowl spots in his career. After his playing days, he remained in Green Bay and became a well-respected broadcaster in the area, and was on hand as an analyst for Super Bowl XLV. The Packers won the game, 31-25, but for McCarren, the similarities of Pittsburgh and Green Bay—communities with deep ties to their football teams—it was the history of the thing that had the most resonance. McCarren played against the great Pittsburgh players of the 1970s dynasty, and then getting an up-close view of the Steelers as they returned four decades later was special.

IT WAS CLASSIC, because you talk about the Steelers and Packers, it's like in hockey with the Original Six. They're part of the fabric of their communities, a lot of people's lives, their fans travel well, they show up all over the country. They have fans all over the country. From a historical perspective, this was a dream matchup, this was what the NFL was all about.

Injuries had been a constant that year, and ironically enough, in the first half of the Super Bowl, (receiver) Donald Driver goes down with the ankle injury. Then (cornerback) Charles Woodson, they lose him just before halftime. This was nothing new to this team, they had been losing guys all year, and I don't think you saw them panic or anything, even as good as Pittsburgh was. The Steelers, you could see, everything was against them early. The first quarter, the Packers go up 14-0 right off the bat. They definitely were caught off guard by that.

But what stood out was that Aaron Rodgers was incredible in that game. He threw for over 300 yards, three touchdowns, no interceptions and despite all of that, he had a number of passes dropped by his receivers. I think for the Steelers, with Rodgers playing like that, it was going to be difficult to keep up with them. And what made it so much harder was that the Packers didn't turn it over a single time, but the Steelers turned it over three times and every one of those led to a Packers score. If your turnover margin is minus-3, it is really hard to win.

Clay Matthews made the big play to force the fumble from (Rashard) Mendenhall to start the fourth quarter, that was the turning point, I think. The Steelers were really kind of catching fire, the momentum was in their favor. Whatever the momentum the Packers had coming out of the first half was all of a sudden gone and it was in the Steelers' favor and Clay makes that hit. The Steelers were driving for a go-ahead score, after all that they had gone through, they had a chance to take the lead. But it was enormous. The Packers got a touchdown out of that and it changed everything.

No question, those last two minutes, you were holding your breath because we all knew what Roethlisberger could do with the game on the line. I think the whole defense was holding its breath. It was tense. The Packers needed a huge defensive series, and they got it. I think it was Tramon Williams with the pass defense to end it on a pass play. When you're six points down, and it's the Super Bowl, and it's Ben Roethlisberger, you're on the edge of your seat. Not until it is fourth down and you see that ball hit the ground do you get off the edge of that seat. They're a touchdown and extra point away from winning that thing. At the end of the day, it was a hell of a Super Bowl. I am sure the Steelers were disappointed and regret the mistakes they made, but as far as just a football game? It was a hell of a Super Bowl.

For me, it was an incredible atmosphere because I had played against Joe Greene, I had played against Jack Ham, Dirt Winston, Jack Lambert, those great linebackers they had. I remember playing in Pittsburgh, and at that time, the Steelers were really good and we were not. You got a sense, starting from the crowd and going to the players, that they don't think they can be beat there. And they were right. We didn't beat him. Everybody talks about home-field advantages, but some places are more of an advantage than others, and Pittsburgh probably has it as much as anyone. I looked around and thought, this is a real-deal home-field advantage.

The Packers have rebuilt that, too. The Green Bay Packers are not just Green Bay, it's the entire state of Wisconsin. It's like the Steelers, the Packers are part of the fabric of their community, their state, people's lives. The Steelers are the same in Western Pennsylvania. When we got back, it was cold, bitter cold, but people were lined up from the airport to the stadium. But if the Steelers had won? I bet it would have been a similar scene in Pittsburgh. That team and the people of that area have a bond. I think part of it is the kind of players they bring in. They're tough. They're smart. They play hard. They have always had that. I don't know how they do it, I don't know where they find these guys. From Joe Greene and Jack Ham to Polamalu and James Harrison and those guys. The names and faces change. But the style, and their ability to make plays and play physical, that doesn't change at all.

You watch the Steelers, and they're synonymous with football and how it should be played. It's got to be part of their DNA.

SECTION 7

EXTRA POINT

CHAPTER 20

DEAR PITTSBURGH STEELER FANS ...

TALK TO JUST about any NFL player or coach, young or old, about the Steelers, and they'll probably bring the conversation around to one clearly distilled fact: the players who were Steelers heroes were a perfect reflection of the city in which they played. Steeler fans are known to travel better than any fan base in pro sports, and their devotion to the black and gold is well documented. What's truly different about the Steelers as a team and Steeler fans as a group is that the steel-town toughness with which they have always been associated shows up in the style of play of their NFL team. Think of Mean Joe Greene ready to take on the entire Denver Broncos bench, think of Mike Webster, sleeveless in negative wind-chill temperatures, think of Rod Woodson and Carnell Lake and Jerome Bettis and Hines Ward and Ben Roethlisberger—there is a grit and a doggedness those players over the years have in common. If that quality is easily recognizable among Pittsburghers, then Pittsburghers should know that for those who went into Pittsburgh as enemy combatants, they recognized the grit and doggedness of the fans as much as they noticed it in the players.

Bill Bergey

I DO REMEMBER ONE time (in 1973), I kind of knocked Terry Bradshaw out of the game, and I hit Terry Hanratty, the backup, pretty hard in the same game. It was the only time I ever got a death threat in my career. I remember thinking, I don't think anyone would ever really do that, but if there was anyone who would do something like that, was going to shoot me, it was probably going to be somebody from Pittsburgh. So every time I went to Pittsburgh, I always had this apprehension that something bad is going to happen here. I remember I even got a police escort from the locker room to the bus because the fans were so irate. And after I had knocked Bradshaw out of the game, I knocked Hanratty out, too, and that is why all those fans in Pittsburgh, it looked like the mob was going to come after me.

But the best thing about playing in Pittsburgh was that you knew you were at a football game. It was not a Tupperware demonstration. They were out for blood, guts, glory, the whole ball of wax. I remember them frothing at the mouth from the moment we pulled up in that bus until we hit that field. It was a football atmosphere all the way. Cincinnati at that time, it was a new football town and it was a conservative place. If you did something good, you would get a little clap. But Pittsburgh fans were in on every play, it was such a big part of their way of life, their way of thinking. I always appreciated that.

John Dutton

ALL THE FANS there, they were crazy. Even when I was in Baltimore, but when I was in Dallas, too—they hated the Cowboys. The Terrible Towel and all of that. They were loud, they were behind their team. It was almost like a college atmosphere. We went in there, and it was the thing where it was the good guys against the bad guys, we were in white and they were in black. So they had a special love-hate thing when we went there. It was just pretty crazy. The atmosphere, even before the game, the place was packed and fans were crazy. So you're dealing with that, and then you go and step on the field at that old place, with the baseball field on it, and it was hard as a rock. The turf was just as if there wasn't any turf, you were just playing on a hard floor.

Sam Wyche

THE FANS IN Pittsburgh were so loud, and really, in our division, in the AFC Central, all the stadiums were really loud. But Pittsburgh was loudest. We came up with a huddle just based on how it was. We were running the no-huddle at that time, and I think the thing was, if you go to Pittsburgh, they were going to be as loud as they possibly could when we had the ball, and nice and quiet when the Steelers had it. That made it difficult for the no-huddle, because so much of it is based on making calls at the line. So we developed the 'sugar' huddle to sort of fight against that, where we quickly huddled at the line, and we were so close to the line they could not risk substituting, because we could snap the ball so quickly. We needed it to play in Cleveland and Houston, too, but Pittsburgh was the loudest, that was the hardest.

Funny, the original title of the sugar huddle was the 'cuddle' huddle, because that was what we were doing—cuddling up at the line. But that lasted all of about six or eight seconds before our guys wanted a new name for it. So I suggested, there is a little colloquialism in the Southeast where I grew up, where you 'sugar up' to your girlfriend. You kind of get close, put your arm around her. So they said, 'OK, let's go with sugar huddle, not cuddle huddle.'

Any place we went where there was a lot of noise, and that was our whole division for a lot of years, we went with the sugar huddle on the road.

Roger Staubach

I THINK BY THAT time, when we played them after the Super Bowl (in 1979), they were a good football team. But it was a tough place to play. L.C. Greenwood knocked me out in that game. But the Pittsburgh fans were actually really good fans. They disliked the Cowboys just like Cowboys fans disliked the Steelers, but I think there was a lot of respect there. I always felt good about Pittsburgh. Whenever I was out at an event, I would say, 'Any Pittsburgh fans out there?' And of course some people would start clapping. And I'd say, 'Yes, those are the folks who pull for the Taliban, too. How could you not pull for America's Team?' I kid with them, but they are really great, loyal fans. I don't have fond memories of the games, but I do have fond memories of the competition and those fans are part of it.

Red Miller

THE CROWD THERE was so tough. It had an effect on you because they'd get so loud and the place would be shaking, you would have to figure out a way to deal with that. The Terrible Towels and all that. If you were behind in the game by a touchdown or something, it felt like you were down by 21 points. Of course, they were such a good team, particularly on the defensive side. But the crowd just added to that. They were such a great fan base, even when we would play them at our place, you would have a lot of Pittsburgh fans there and you would say, 'Where did all these people come from?'

John Dinkel

PLAYING IN THREE Rivers was definitely memorable. It was like you were playing in front of a bunch of clones. It was the 1970s, and everybody had long, dark hair. It was Pittsburgh, so they all had moustaches. I don't want to be too stereotypical but it was the look. You would look up in the crowd and all the fans looked alike, sometimes even the women. They had, at both Three Rivers and Riverfront, they had these old polka bands, the oompah bands and knowing the heritage of both teams, people lived and died for those games. I loved road trips in the NFL, but going to Pittsburgh, you would get so jacked up because the fans were that way, too. You had to try to beat the fans, and you had to try to beat the players. The Steelers were awesome like that.

Ross Browner

MY SON MAX (Starks) played for them, he was with them for nine years. So of course, I had to become a Steeler fan in the process, and going back to watch those Steelers games in Pittsburgh, it was funny how it brought back so many memories. Those Terrible Towels waving all over the place, they were so, so loud, it was always difficult to go play there. And you had it so that, even in your own home games, those fans were so eager to support their team that they would travel in big droves, so our home games were sometimes a lot like Steelers home games, if you know what I mean. It was wonderful having Max play for them—my Bengals fans were not happy with me wearing Steelers gear, but I would just say, 'Yeah, but that's my son out there.'

Bobby Ross

IT IS EASY to go in there and feel intimidated by it. I would always talk to my team about that, whenever we played in Pittsburgh. They had the Terrible Towel thing there, and that was something that could be distracting if you let it be. You walk in the stadium and they take the field and all you see is yellow. Obviously, structurally, you had to be concerned about your communication, offensively and defensively as well. I think we handled that, I don't think we had any delay of game penalties. We practiced it, crowd noise and that type of thing.

But that was a big factor, it can be intimidating, because you have these 80,000 people in the stadium and it is not just any people, it was Pittsburgh people. I think everyone knows the people from Pittsburgh are known for being tough. Heck, when I was a college coach at Maryland, I would always try to go up there and get a couple of Pittsburgh guys because you knew they were going to be tough. When I played in college, I played with guys from Sturgeon, Pa., Dunbar, Pa., Pitcairn, Pa. I mean, those guys were all the same way—they were tougher than hell. I always thought it started with the toughness that the people in Pittsburgh exhibit, and it carries over to the football team. The thing we had to fight when we were in San Diego was that we were soft because we were out there in that beautiful weather, no rain, no snow, so we had to fight that. That was why playing Pittsburgh was so important for us. If you want to add toughness to your team, you need to beat the Steelers. You need to go to Pittsburgh.

INDEX

The following individuals were interviewed for Facing the Pittsburgh Steelers. *Their comments appear on the pages below.*